HOW TO IMPROVE MEMORY QUICKLY BY KNOWING YOUR PERSONAL MEMORY STYLE

QUICK, EASY TIPS TO IMPROVE MEMORY THROUGH THE BRAIN'S FASTEST SUPERLINKS MEMORY AND LEARNING STYLE

RICKI LINKSMAN

.

HOW TO IMPROVE MEMORY QUICKLY BY KNOWING YOUR PERSONAL MEMORY STYLE

QUICK, EASY TIPS TO IMPROVE MEMORY THROUGH THE BRAIN'S FASTEST SUPERLINKS MEMORY AND LEARNING STYLE

HOW TO IMPROVE MEMORY QUICKLY
BY KNOWING YOUR PERSONAL MEMORY STYLE
Copyright © 1996-2016 Ricki Linksman

This edition published 2016 by
National Reading Diagnostics Institute,
Naperville, Illinois

ISBN: 978-1-928997-90-0

PRAISE FOR RICKI LINKSMAN'S BOOKS
AND BRAIN-BASED LEARNING METHODS

From Publications:

From "Woman News," New York, New York:
"There is a way to learn anything you want rapidly and successfully. The technique can be applied to any sort of learning in any field you choose. Each of us has a Superlink— the easiest method for us to fully learn information. Once you've found your Superlink, you can use it to learn in ways that are easy, effortless, and automatic." —published in an article in New York's "Woman News" called, "Mind Power: Smarten Up! Tap into Your Brain's Superlink—Learning Becomes Easy, Effortless, and Automatic"

From "L.A. Parent" and "San Diego Parent," California:
"All children in California will be reading at grade level or above by the end of third grade.' With this promise, California state leaders have made reading instruction in the early grades (K through Grade 3) a top priority in the public schools. So while the politicians are trying to do their part, how can parents help their little readers measure up? According to Ricki Linksman, author of *Your Child Can Be a Great Reader*, parents should first figure out their child's learning style.

i

"Research shows that each of us receives information in different ways. Visual learners learn best through their eyes, auditory learners through their ears, tactile learners by touching, and kinesthetic learners by moving around."

–From an article in the "L.A. Times" and "San Diego Times," called "What is Your Child's Reading Style? If You Know How Your Child Reads You Can Help Him/Her Learn," by Judy Molland

Family Time Magazine:
Feb. 2007, published an article about how Keys to Reading Success™ helped two local suburban Chicago area schools (Fairmont and East Aurora) meet state standards.

From the Iowa "Gazette," Cedar Rapids, Iowa:
"Author Ricki Linksman has plenty of tips for parents who want to be sure their kids love to read, and can read well."

From the "Abilene Reporter-News," Abilene, Texas:
"This step-by-step guide is designed to help children overcome every kind of reading problem and get back up to grade level or beyond. It is filled with short, fun activities to do at home and provides pointers to boost self-esteem and motivation." (Jan. 24, 1999)

From a Public School District Superintendent:

"Ricki Linksman has synthesized the educational research into concepts which makes learning accessible to anyone. While the term differentiation of instruction is very popular in the world of education, Ricki Linksman provides concrete examples and techniques of combining learning styles with brain hemispheric preference to create an individualized "superlink." These techniques are personalized to open the pathways for anyone to learn anything quickly. For example, our junior high school went from 2/3 of the students below state level on state reading assessment tests to 2/3 of the students above state level in reading within eight months."

–Dr. Michael Early, Public School District Superintendent, Illinois, and former School Principal in West Suburban Chicago

From a School Superintendent:

"This is the only reading program I have found with the scientifically-based reading research that has proven statistics to raise reading levels so rapidly. Keys to Reading Success™ helped our school get off the state watch list that it had been on for 6 years, and this year—2006—we have finally made AYP or met state reading standards by using the program for only 6 months. The discipline problems in our school have been dramatically reduced as students went from reading below grade level to reading above grade level within 6 months. They are engaged in learning and have raised their self-esteem and motivation to achieve in school. Its parent involvement lessons in all learning styles and brain styles allow parents and teachers to work as a team for every child's success. This program ensures that every student can raise reading levels and test scores by Keys to Reading Success's™ comprehensive but easy-to-use reading diagnosis, learning styles and brain styles assessment, and its powerful, effective, and engaging teacher reading lesson plans in all learning styles. Using learning styles has helped every student learn to read in his or her most effective and fastest learning style possible."

**–Dr. Doris Langon, Superintendent,
Fairmont District 89, Lockport, Illinois.**

From a District School Superintendent on Gains in High School, Middle School, and Elementary School, including Indian Oaks Academy for Special Needs:
"Through using this program, significant gains were made in our district in elementary, middle, and high school on the CTBS (Cognitive Test of Basic Skills) test. Our ISAT (Illinois Standards Achievement Test) scores in reading showed significant growth. Gains in reading ranged from 1-8 grade levels in 9 months in the elementary, middle, and high school grades. From 86%-99% of students in grades 1-5 accelerated to read from 1-8 years above grade level in reading within 9

months (including Regular Ed and Special Ed students). In the middle school, students rose from 1-6 years above grade level. In the high school 99.5% of students grades 9-12 rose from 1-2 grade levels in reading in 9 months."

–M.S., Asst. Supt. Curriculum, Manteno School District

From a Principal of a Charter School in East Los Angeles, California:

"East Los Angeles school, Culture and Language Academy of Success (CLAS), a charter school devoted to African-American culture in the Los Angeles Unified School District rose from not meeting State Standards in reading to exceeding state standards in reading in 1 year using Ricki Linksman's *Keys to Reading Success* program using the techniques in *How to Learn Anything Quickly*. On a scale from 200-1000, they reached 773, with 35 points gain, and came close to the 800 superior school status. LA Unified District only reached 600 with a 9-point gain in 1 year. CLAS achieved 773, while California's state average was 635."

–Principal, Dr. Sharroky Hollie,
CLAS Charter School, Los Angeles, California

From a School Principal at Dieterich School in District 131, East Aurora, Illinois:

"With 83% of the school population speaking only Spanish and being enrolled in the English Language Learners (ELL) program, Dieterich School in East Aurora, Illinois, scored as the third highest in the district in their reading scores on the March 2006 ISAT Illinois State Achievement Test) reading test using Keys to Reading Success™ and Superlinks to Accelerated Learning™, using techniques from *How to Learn Anything Quickly*."

**–Principal, Dieterich Elementary School,
East Aurora, Illinois**

From an Elementary School:
"2/3 of the students in grades 1-3 rose from 1-7 grade levels in reading above grade level in one school year."

–M.S., Teacher, Elementary School in Joliet, Illinois

From a Technology Director:
"We need to get past the assembly line way we teach and test. Through the use of technology and the Keys to Reading Success program, teachers can easily manage "progressive monitoring," diagnostic testing and reporting for students on an individual basis. This in turn allows teachers to customize each student's learning needs...what could be better?"

**-Vicki Dewitt, Technology Hub Director,
Edwardsville, Illinois**

From Learning Identity, South Africa:
"Ricki Linksman has a heart to make a difference in the lives of those who struggle with reading. She has developed a unique learning and reading program based on brain

processing and learning styles, which undertakes to teach ANYONE how to read and learn and most importantly how to comprehend the content matter. We have had remarkable success with 100's of students utilizing Ricki's Keys to Reading Success and Superlinks to Accelerated Learning program, and consider it an honor to be a part of her work."

–Trish Gatland, Learning Identity, South Africa

From Sports Coaches and Trainers:

From a Head Football Coach:

"Using these accelerated learning techniques such as teaching through learning styles has helped our university football team have its first winning season ever. The athletes learned the plays faster and better through these techniques. We also had our best academic year ever, for our academic support to our athletes."

–Ken Karcher, University Head Football Coach

From a Graduate of the National Academy of Sports Medicine (NASM) Certified Personal Trainer program:

"I passed the National Academy of Sports Medicine (NASM) Certified Personal Trainer (CPT) exam. The NASM CPT is considered the Cadillac of certifications for Personal Fitness Trainers and the exam has a notoriously high failure rate. The course itself (almost all correspondence based) is exceptionally detailed oriented and requires students to learn everything from intricate human anatomy to psychology, and everything in between. If I had known how hard it was going to be when I set out to do it, I don't think I would have even attempted it! While not all certifications are equal, those who have done the NASM CPT course and passed are in my opinion, border level scientists. Having done it myself, my respect level has gone through the roof not just for other NASM Certified Personal Trainers but also for myself. I wanted to let you know how grateful I am to you for all you did for me in learning about myself, my learning style (highly kinesthetic) and how to work around potential roadblocks. I have since learned even more about what makes me "tick." It's an exciting journey! Ricki, I wanted to take the time out to thank you from the bottom of my heart for everything you did for me--I don't think any of my success would have been possible without your help and expertise."

–Skye Middleton, NASM Certified Personal Trainer

From Teachers Who Took the Master's Degree
Teacher Education Superlinks Courses:

"In that one year, I learned more about teaching reading than from my entire college education."

–M.S., Teacher, Farragut Elementary School, Joliet,
Illinois

"The teacher training in reading is the best I have ever taken."
–Special Education Teacher,
Naperville Consolidated School District #203, Illinois

"The course in how to teach reading stretched my thinking about learning. The material was practical, hands-on, and relevant. Excellent trainer. It is the best course I have taken in years."
–High School Title 1 Reading Teacher,
Downers South High School, Downers Grove, Illinois

"I now have some tools and tests to evaluate why some of my students are not learning and to have techniques to teach to all my students. I recommend that every teacher take this training--it will open your eyes and hearts."
–Teacher, Aurora Public Schools, Illinois

From Adult Learners:

"I am 26 years old and throughout my school career was labeled dyslexic. I never learned to read and ended up with a job and career that did not interest me. I wanted to go to college. Within 6 months of using Ricki Linksman's accelerated learning techniques, I learned to read well enough to pass the college entrance examination, and have been admitted to a college that will prepare me for the career I want."
–A.L., Chicago

"I am in my 50's and could never read. Through the Superlinks learning style and brain style test, I discovered that I had never been able to learn to read before because the method used in the school when I was growing up did not match the way I needed to learn. Working with Ricki Linksman and her accelerated learning techniques, I learned how to read in my best learning style and I can now enjoy books. Ricki then donated her services for free to our local branch of the *Literacy Volunteer of America* to train tutors in her Keys to Reading Success™ reading comprehension and memory program so they could keep working with adults who wanted to learn to read."

–J.S., Chicago

I had purchased Ricki's earlier book, *How to Learn Anything Quickly: Quick, Easy Tips to Improve Memory, Reading Comprehension, Test-Taking Skills, and Learning through the Brain's Fastest Superlinks Learning Style* a year ago when I was starting a study-at-home Medical Transcription program. At first, I somehow did not get past the first two pages. It ended up tucked in the bottom of my nightstand drawer. (I am a tactile-mixed with left-side dominate learner). Three weeks ago, after struggling with comprehension and memory, I bit the bullet and got an extension. But, more importantly, I decided to commit to reading the book. Wow, I am glad I picked it up and forced myself to push past the first few pages. I have not been able to put it down, and will be finishing it up today. It was a really eye opening to see that the teaching styles of my teachers varied in my primary, elementary, high school, and college experiences. I passed Biology and Psychology with flying colors, but could not seem to get a passing grade from Nutrition class. Of course, with your confidence shattered, you never see the parallels. You never look at the classes you did pass and wonder what went wrong; you just give up. (Or label yourself). How sobering to know that it was not my lack of ability; it was the learning style in which the information was presented—that each teacher had his or her own way of presenting the material, and it was the teachers that taught closer to my learning style where I excelled the most. I have a renewed commitment to complete my at-home study course and will take all that I have learned in this book with me throughout my life, for every subject I wish to learn. I have also bought two more copies for my husband and sister. This letter is just a huge thank you for writing such an easy to understand book, full of knowledge that can change anyone who is curious how to improve their learning and memory. Thank you!

–D.H., adult learner

From a Title 1 Success Story:
A 1st grader was not reading on level by mid-first grade. The parents and teachers were so concerned that they wanted to do an evaluation to see if he had a learning disability. During the waiting period for his evaluation, the Keys to Reading Success Accelerated Phonics Program was used with him in his Title 1 class. It was discovered that he was a kinesthetic

learner. He used the kinesthetic component of the Keys to Reading Success Accelerated Phonics Program, and within months, mastered all the phonetic patterns and was not only able to read well at a 1st grade level, but accelerated into 2nd grade level reading, while still a first grader. By the time he was evaluated by the psychologist, they discovered he actually had an I.Q. in the 140's and he was then placed in a gifted program. Had we not discovered his learning style and taught him through that method, he may have fallen even further behind in his reading level and it may have taken years to find out that he did not have a learning disability.

From University Instructors:

"Every teacher should use Keys to Reading Success. It is the most complete program of reading available. It is an excellent training tool for new teachers."

**–College Instructor for Graduate Education Courses
for Teachers, Benedictine University, Lisle, Illinois**

From Parents Who Used the Superlinks Methods with Their Children and Teens:

"My high school son was getting D's and F's, but after a reading diagnosis and learning style assessment from Keys to Reading Success and receiving instruction in study skills and memory skills in his learning style, he is now getting A's. The program has also helped him on his SATs and ACTs."

–M.O., Parent, Naperville, Illinois

"When we started coming to Ricki Linksman at National Reading Diagnostics Institute, my son was in first grade, but reading at a kindergarten level, and his self-confidence was down. After working with Ricki for the past 11 months using her Keys to Reading Success™, Superlinks to Accelerated Learning™, and Off the Wall Phonics™ program, his reading level has improved so much that he is wanting to read books and complete Accelerated Reader™ book tests at school. My son is enjoying reading now that he reads at grade level and we will continue to work with Ricki to get him past grade level. What a difference! Even his teacher in school has noticed and commented, 'He is to be commended for reading and taking tests on 23 books this quarter! He's starting to enjoy reading, which is wonderful.'"

–L.M., Wheaton Christian Grammar School, Winfield, Illinois

"My child has made tremendous gains in a short time. His self-esteem has risen dramatically."

–A.P., Parent, Naperville

"My 10th grade son went from grades of 'F's" and 'D's' to 'A's' in 4 weeks. His study skills, comprehension, and memory has improved tremendously."

–Parent, Westmont

"In 6 months, my 4th grade child, who was reading 3 years below level, came up to grade level and is doing well in school."

–Parent, Lisle

"I have learned so much about how to help my son and about learning styles in general. I have to say that the frustration level when doing homework or reading has gone down dramatically.

–M.H., Chicago

"We have seen improved results in my son's tests and overall academics. In fact, he made the honor roll!! I appreciate the fact she is able to see how he best comprehends his reading material and incorporates the best plan for him. We are very happy to see his overall comprehension improve and especially his confidence. Thank you, Ricki!"

–L.Z., parent

"My kindergartener is now reading 3rd grade books, and doing addition, subtraction, multiplication, and division over several months' time."

–Mr. R.M., Parent, Naperville

"For the first time, my 2nd grader could read on his grade level, and his self-esteem has increased tremendously."

–Parent, Chicago

"We wanted our 4-year-old child to qualify for a gifted school but she didn't achieve the necessary score on her first test. Within less than a year, she not only learned to read at a 3rd grade level, but was able to qualify for the gifted school. We are so thrilled with the results."

–S.D., Parent, Wheaton

"I home school my children and I learned how to accelerate their reading at home."

–Parent, Batavia

"My gifted child loves the challenging activities."

–Parent, Downers Grove

"I've looked for years for help for my son and Ricki Linksman is the only person that came through. My son has made more progress in these last 8 months than he has K through 6th grade. She provides concrete solutions to his specific areas that he needs help in. I recommend Ricki's book to anyone whose child is struggling at school or who wants to give their child an advantage to succeed. Ricki has not only helped my son to learn but his attitude and confidence has increased dramatically. I have seen amazing results for my son. Not only has his reading level improved dramatically but his confidence and enthusiasm are through the roof!"

–S.S., Parent, Illinois

"If you are reading this, you are probably concerned about the progress your child or grandchild is making in learning to read. I was in the same position several years ago. My grandson wasn't learning to read in his school. He had been left back in the same grade twice because he could not read. He was diagnosed with ADD and a learning disability. We spent years trying to find out why he could not read because he was a bright boy. As a concerned parent or grandparent, I got on the Internet and found Ricki Linksman's National Reading Diagnostics Institute and its Keys to Reading Success® and its Superlinks to Accelerated Learning™ programs which determined what his learning style and brain hemispheric preference was. The assessment determined he was a kinesthetic and tactile learner with a right brain hemispheric preference. It gave us a prescriptive plan to solve the problem and lessons in his best learning style. Within the first lesson of Keys to Reading Success®, using kinesthetic right brain learning techniques, my grandson read for the first time in his life, to his joy and excitement. After only one session with the Keys to Reading Success® materials, I watched this little guy read solid first-grade material that he had never been able to read before for the first time in his life. Yet, several hours before that first session, he had not even known the letters of the alphabet. I almost fell out of my chair, I was so excited. I knew then that I was on the right track, and I had found the right person and right techniques and program to teach this young lad how to read. He has been reading ever since. Within a few months, he was able to read at his grade level, and we were able to take him off his ADD medication. We now know what works for him and we attributed it to National Reading Diagnostics Institute and Keys to Reading Success. The developer of Keys to Reading Success®, Ricki Linksman, is truly the Michael Jordan of reading."

–Rusty Acree, Concerned Grandparent,
Retd. Naval Officer, and Field Judge for University
Football Games, Richmond, Virginia

And from his grandson, who wrote: When asked about what he liked best about his trip to Chicago, the lad wrote: "Learning to read. Thank you, Mrs. Linksman."

"Our teenager did not score well on the practice test for a high school entrance exam to Benet Academy, a college preparatory school. After a few months of work at National Reading Diagnostics Institute, areas of need were targeted and our teen got 99% on the actual entrance exam and was admitted to the preparatory school."

–Parent, Lisle

"Our son was in special education classes since 1st grade and by 7th grade still had not learned to read. We brought him to Ricki Linksman for a reading diagnosis and she gave him a Keys to Reading Success® reading diagnostic test, Superlinks™ learning style and brain style test, and tutoring instruction.

Our son learned to read in months and no longer needed to be in special education. His self-esteem has gone up and he is so happy now."

–B. Burke., Parent, Miami, Florida

"My high school sophomore never dropped below A's or B's before, so when he dropped to a C in English, we were beside ourselves with frustration. After using these strategies for only 6 weeks, he not only went back up to A, but was the only student in the class to receive a writing award!"

–M.H., Parent

"We did not feel our middle school son had the skills to be ready for high school. He was struggling in many of his school subjects and even needed audios to read his assigned books to him. After only two months using these strategies, he can now read by himself, and his grades have improved to the point where the principal and teachers are astounded by his amazing progress! He feels proud of himself, enjoys school now, and has boosted his vocabulary, memory, study skills, and test-taking skills. The best part is that he does not need to be read to, but can read at and above his grade level all by himself!

–K.A., Parent

"My daughter struggled with reading in early elementary school, and I realized that when she read to me, she was only memorizing the book and could not read on her own. Ricki Linksman at National Reading Diagnostics Institute gave the Superlinks test and found out she was a kinesthetic right brain learner and the techniques in her school were not matching how she best learned. By using kinesthetic right brain techniques for her learning. Ricki not only taught her to read at grade level within a few months, but raised her several years above her age as well. Throughout the rest of her school career, she became a top reader and student in her class, no longer needed tutoring, and ended up in honors classes. In high school, she was number eleven in overall standing in her school. She returned to National Reading Diagnostics Institute to work with Ricki Linksman for ACT test prep, in her kinesthetic right brain learning style, and got a perfect score on the English ACT! She not only gained admission to numerous universities, but she was offered several scholarships, won academic awards, and ended up selecting a college, whose scholarship is paying $25,000.00 a year for each of the four years for her tuition. We are so glad we found National Reading Diagnostics Institute and Ricki Linksman and recommend her to any parent who wants to lay the foundation early for their child's future success in high school, college, and in life."

–J.O., Parent, Wheaton, Illinois

Awards and Achievements:

IASCD (Illinois Association for Supervision and Curriculum Development) awarded a WINN Research Certificate of Award of Merit for Outstanding Research to Ricki Linksman, Developer of Keys to Reading Success, for "Maximizing Reading Growth in Nine Months from 2-5 Grade Levels by Using Accelerated Phonics Taught through Learning Styles."

OTHER BOOKS AND RESOURCES
BY THE AUTHOR, RICKI LINKSMAN

Books, eBooks, and Software about the Brain; Memory Improvement; Accelerated Learning through Learning Styles and Brain Styles; Kinesthetic, Tactile, Visual, Auditory Left and Right Brain Learners; Reading and Listening Comprehension Strategies; Accelerated Phonics; Vocabulary; Test-taking, Note-taking, and Study Skills and Test Prep for High School and College Entrance Exams, (ACT, SAT); Self-Esteem; Motivation; Concentration; and Focus

How to Learn Anything Quickly: Quick, Easy Tips to Improve Memory, Reading Comprehension, Test-Taking Skills, and Learning through the Brain's Fastest Superlinks Learning Style

How to Improve Memory Quickly: Quick, Easy Tips to Improve Memory through the Brain's Fastest Superlinks Learning Style

The Fine Line between ADHD and Kinesthetic Learners: 197 Kinesthetic Activities to Quickly Improve Reading, Memory, and Learning in Just 10 Weeks: The Ultimate Parent Guide to ADD, ADHD, and Kinesthetic Learners

How to Improve Reading Comprehension Quickly by Knowing Your Personal Reading Comprehension Style: Quick, Easy Tips to Improve Comprehension through the Brain's Fastest Superlinks Learning Style

Solving Your Child's Reading Problem

From ADHD or ADD to A's: Improve Reading, Memory, and Learning Quickly for Kinesthetic Learners

The Power of Mental Golf, by Kerry Graham, past LPGA president, and Ricki Linksman

Your Child Can Be a Great Reader

Keys to Reading Success™: Internet Reading Program (includes Linksman Passage Reading Tests, Linksman Phonics Diagnostic Test, and Superlinks Assessment, plus 1000s of pages of reading lesson plans in all learning styles: Kinesthetic, Tactile, Visual, and Auditory with adaptations for right and left brain learners in reading comprehension, phonics, vocabulary, test-taking strategies, test prep, and study skills.

Superlinks to Accelerated Learning Assessment™ (includes Linksman Learning Style Preference Assessment™ and Linksman Brain Hemispheric Preference Assessment™)

Off the Wall Phonics (Accelerated K-12, College, and Adult Phonics Program to Improve Reading Comprehension, Word

Reading and Fluency for Kinesthetic, Tactile, Visual, and Auditory Learners, both Right Brain and Left Brain Learners)

Kinesthetic, Tactile, Visual, and Auditory Learners, both Right-Brain and Left-Brain Learners)

Kinesthetic Vocabulary Activities Your Child Will Love
Tactile Vocabulary Activities Your Child Will Love

How to Quickly Improve Memory and Learning for Kinesthetic Left and Right Brain Superlinks Learning Styles

How to Quickly Improve Memory and Learning for Tactile Left and Right Brain Superlinks Learning Styles

How to Quickly Improve Memory and Learning for Visual Left and Right Brain Superlinks Learning Styles

How to Quickly Improve Memory and Learning for Auditory Left and Right Brain Superlinks Learning Styles

How to Quickly Improve Reading Comprehension for Kinesthetic Left and Right Brain Superlinks Learning Styles

How to Quickly Improve Reading Comprehension for Tactile Left and Right Brain Superlinks Learning Styles

How to Quickly Improve Reading Comprehension for Visual Left and Right Brain Superlinks Learning Styles

How to Quickly Improve Reading Comprehension for Auditory Left and Right Brain Superlinks Learning Styles

How to Quickly Improve Study, Note-taking and Test- taking Skills for Kinesthetic Left and Right Brain Superlinks Learning Styles

How to Quickly Improve Study, Note-taking and Test- taking Skills for Tactile Left and Right Brain Superlinks Learning Styles

How to Quickly Improve Study, Note-taking and Test- taking Skills for Visual Left and Right Brain Superlinks Learning Styles

How to Quickly Improve Study, Note-taking and Test- taking Skills for Auditory Left and Right Brain Superlinks Learning Styles

Vowel and Consonant Guide

Superlinks to Accelerated Learning: Phonics Diagnostic Test

For other products, books, eBooks, software, trainings, and e-courses visit:

www.readinginstruction.com
www.keyslearning.com
www.superlinkslearning.com
www.keystoreadingsuccesss.com
or e-mail: info@keyslearning.com

Special note to the reader: This book is part of a series. Other books in the series include: improving reading comprehension; and improving study, note-taking, and test-taking skills for learning any subject. If you want one book that contains all the books in the series combined in the full compendium than you can buy: *How to Learn Anything Quickly: Quick, Easy Tips to Improve Memory, Reading Comprehension, and Test- taking Skills through the Brain's Fastest Superlinks Learning Style.*

Dedicated to
all those who devote their lives to
helping others achieve their goals in life.

TABLE OF CONTENTS

INTRODUCTION

You can improve your memory to remember *everything* you read and learn quickly. Applying brain research to teaching people how to improve their memory for the past thirty years, people of all ages have used these quick, easy, and fun tips and strategies to achieve success in the shortest possible time. Whether you want to use your memory power for school, college, job, career, sports, or hobbies, you can become a memory whiz. You do not have to wait for months or years to learn these secrets to improving memory quickly—they are available now within this book for anyone to use to learn anything for any purpose.

When I published my book, *How to Learn Anything Quickly: Quick, Easy Tips to Improve Memory, Reading Comprehension, and Test-taking Skills through the Brain's Fastest Superlinks Learning Style*, many people asked me if I could just do a book focused only on memory, especially adults who aim to keep their memory active and strong as they age. Others felt they wanted a simple handbook to help them with challenges such as learning a new job or going back to school.

Coaches, professors, teachers, and trainers also want techniques to help those they are teaching or training accelerate their speed of remembering the material. I decided to publish this short handbook focused on memory with quick, easy strategies anyone can use.

Special note to the reader: This book is part of a series. Other books in the series include: improving reading comprehension;

and improving study, note-taking, and test-taking skills for learning any subject. If you want one book that contains all the books in the series combined in the full compendium than you can buy: *How to Learn Anything Quickly: Quick, Easy Tips to Improve Memory, Reading Comprehension, and Test-taking Skills through the Brain's Fastest Superlinks Learning Style.*

After using and testing these revolutionary brain-based memory methods for decades with corporations, businesses, sports teams, universities, colleges, elementary, middle, and high school districts, and with individuals, students, parents, and families, I have tracked how these strategies have consistently proven to take any learner to success within days, weeks, and months—not years! Now, I share with you in this book those same quick, easy tips to increase your memory to learn anything quickly. Use your brain's energy powers to succeed in the competitive job market, whether to get hired for a job, keep your job, or keep pace with new information and technology in a rapidly-changing job market. *How to Improve Memory Quickly* gives you fast, simple, and powerful memory strategies to remember *everything* you read and learn for rapid success.

Since the 1970s I have applied brain-based teaching methods to help people of all ages (pre-K, kindergarten, grades 1-12, college, and adult) use their brain's unique Superlinks learning style and brain style to improve memory quickly and successfully. These powerful techniques, proven for over 35 years in school districts, colleges, corporations, businesses, and sports teams have helped people become top students and workers in the shortest possible time. Among those who been successful using these memory techniques are:

- Adult learners from college to post-graduate school to raise grades and improve reading comprehension, vocabulary, note taking, study skills, and test-taking skills
- Baby-boomers and seniors to exercise their brain and memory for lifelong learning
- Adults in the job market needing to rapidly learn new information and skills to find or keep a job, pass certification tests, start a new career when downsized, or keep pace with rapidly changing technology in the workplace
- Parents to help their child or teen (pre-K, kindergarten, grades 1- 12, or college, whether in regular education, special education, gifted, honors, bilingual, ESL, ELL, dual language program, Title 1, or Remedial Reading programs, or who have ADHD or ADD) improve memory for reading comprehension, note taking, study and test-taking skills, concentration, focus, and self-esteem, and raise grades, reading levels, and test scores for state or standardized tests or high school or college placement tests (i.e., ACT or SAT) in the shortest possible time.
- Teachers, college instructors, coaches, or trainers to teach students or trainees in their fastest Superlinks learning style and brain style for mastery.
- Doctors, psychologists, psychiatrists, social workers, and therapists to give clients tools to reduce stress-related illnesses from fear of school or test taking by giving them confidence to learn and remember anything.

- Football, baseball, basketball, soccer, hockey, or golf coaches who want their athletes to rapidly learn and memorize their sports playbook or skills and keep up academic grades
- Spanish-speaking students or those who speak any other language to rapidly learn English, or English-speaking students who want to know how to learn and remember *any* language quickly
- Anyone wanting to improve relationships and communication skills with family, spouses, significant others, friends, or co-workers or employees, whether a visual, auditory, tactile, kinesthetic, or left-brain or right- brain learner to understand themselves and others and how they remember information.

It has been heart-warming and rewarding to receive feedback from people of all ages throughout the world that these simple, easy methods to increase memory have transformed their lives by helping them achieve success in any field—quickly. My hope is that all readers of this book, *How to Improve Memory Quickly by Knowing Your Personal Memory Style: Quick, Easy Tips to Improve Memory through the Brain's Fastest Superlinks Memory and Learning Style,* unlock your own amazing brain power, experience the joy of learning, raise your confidence and self-esteem, and help you attain success starting right now in whatever area you wish to achieve in life!

–Ricki Linksman

PART 1:
INCREASE YOUR MEMORY
THROUGH BRAIN-BASED METHODS

CHAPTER 1:
HOW TO IMPROVE YOUR MEMORY QUICKLY

Do you want to keep your memory sharp? Are you concerned whether your memory will stay strong as you become older? Do you wish to increase your memory to learn any subject quickly? Are you a job seeker or employee looking for a new job and must learn how to learn and remember new skills fast? Do you need to improve your memory to learn study skills, note taking, and test-taking skills to prepare for a career certification test, college boards, or placement exam but it has been a long time since you last used these skills in school that you need a quick refresher? Do you find it hard to keep up with change? Are constant innovations at your place of employment forcing you to spend time continually learning and remembering new skills or learning to use new technological equipment? Do you wish you had the memory power to learn the skills required at your job more rapidly?

Do you wish you could better remember what you study and read? Are you frustrated by having to spend more time rereading because you cannot remember what you read or learned the first time? Do you feel so hopeless that you do not think you can remember much at all?

Take heart! You can successfully improve your memory quickly to learn anything you want. This book can help anyone of any age, whether you are:

- a senior citizen or baby-boomer who want to increase your memory and keep it sharp
- a job seeker who want to remember information for a job or career

7

- a teacher who wants teaching methods, techniques, and strategies to help your students improve memory for better grades or test scores
- a parent who wants to improve your child or teen's grades
- a student who wants to improve your memory for better reading comprehension, study skills, note taking, or test-taking skills for the ACT or SAT, state reading tests, high school placement test, or college boards
- a parent who wants to know how to raise a gifted and talented child with strong memory skills from the time he or she is a baby or toddler
- a trainer or employer who wants to be more effective in helping trainees or employees remember their new job skills
- a sports coach who wants your football, basketball, baseball, soccer, golf, gymnastics, or hockey players to learn and remember the sports play book faster and better and help your athletes improve
- a person who wants to learn how to remember new vocabulary words in Spanish, French, German, Chinese, or any language for school, a job, or a career
- a person of any age who needs to learn and remember English vocabulary words
- an adult who wants to improve relationships and communication skills by knowing how others remember
- a supervisor, employer, employee, co-worker, or customer who wants to communicate better with others on the job by knowing how they remember best

- a doctor, psychiatrist, psychologist, or social worker who wants to help clients and patients improve their memories
- anyone who has a hobby, skill, or passion you want to pursue and learn and remember quickly.

This book gives you fast, easy strategies to help you improve your memory quickly.

Advances in science, particularly neuroscience, have helped us better understand the way our brain works. Although this knowledge has been in laboratories, research centers, and scientific journals for years, few people have applied it to make our everyday life easier.

Some of these advances have gradually become public knowledge over the past few decades. Unfortunately, many educational institutions throughout the world are still in the dark ages when it comes to these advanced brain-based learning techniques. This book gives every person a method to learn and remember successfully and quickly. It is user-friendly and simple to follow. It is written for everyone: for people of all ages, at all levels of education, and is designed to help every person improve memory quickly.

You will learn strategies and techniques to rapidly improve your memory that can be applied to any field you choose. Once you have improved your memory you will be able to use these methods for the rest of your life for anything you wish to remember. This book will help you find the path to increasing your memory in a way that works best for you.

Follow the fast, easy, and simple steps in the book and you will emerge from the last page of this book an expert on how *you* remember best and how to apply it to any field you want.

What Is a Memory Learning Style, Brain Hemispheric Preference, or Your Best Memory Superlink?

What is a memory learning style, a brain hemispheric preference, or a memory superlink? We each have a different way of learning and remembering. Each of us has a memory *superlink* that makes remembering anything faster, easier, and more comfortable. Your memory superlink is the easiest method for you to improve your memory of information in order to understand it, remember it, and retain it; it links to our brain information we want to remember in a superfast way. Your memory superlink is a combination of your best learning style and the part of the brain you use to process and store information. Each of us learns and remembers differently. Some remember best what they read, whereas others remember best what they hear. Your memory learning style is the way you receive information from the world. What are the four main memory learning styles? The main ways of learning and remembering are visual, auditory, tactile, and kinesthetic, or a combination of these. **Visual learners** remember best through seeing, either printed or graphic material, or their surroundings. **Auditory learners** remember best by hearing, listening, and talking. **Tactile learners** remember best through tactile sensation and by touching objects, experiencing information through their feelings, or using their hands and fingers. **Kinesthetic learners** remember best by doing action and moving their large motor muscles. Some people use two, three, or all four memory learning style modalities to remember.

After we use our memory learning style to comprehend information, our brain processes and stores the information either using the left side (left hemisphere) of the brain or the right side (right hemisphere) or a combination of the two. Each side has a different comprehension and memory style, or its own way of thinking about and looking at the world. Some of us have a **left-brain hemispheric preference** and some have a **right-brain hemispheric preference**, while some use both sides of the brain. **Left-brain learners** tend to be sequential and remember information in a linear manner. **Right-brain learners** tend to remember globally, seeing the big picture, and connecting seemingly unrelated ideas. Also, left-brain learners remember better in symbols such as letters, words, and numbers, while right-brain learners remember better using sensory images of sights, sounds, smell, tastes, and touch, and movement, without words.

By determining *your* memory learning style and *your* brain hemispheric preference, you can find your memory superlink—your fastest style of remembering. There are eight Superlinks memory learning styles and brain styles to improve memory: **visual left-brain, visual right-brain, auditory left-brain, auditory right-brain, tactile left-brain, tactile right-brain, kinesthetic left-brain, and kinesthetic right-brain.**

When someone is instructing us in a different way than the one that matches our best style, it is uncomfortable, unnatural, and stressful, and we do not learn and remember as effectively and quickly. For example, think about the hand you use for writing. You have become so used to using that hand that it has become automatic; you do not even think about it.

However, if you were asked to write with the opposite hand, it may be difficult, awkward, slower, and uncomfortable. You could *force* yourself to use that hand, but

11

it would be a struggle. You would be so busy concentrating on getting your hand to write that you may not even be able to focus on what it is you are supposed to be writing. It is the same with our memory learning style. When we remember through our memory superlink, remembering is fast, easy, effortless, and automatic. When we remember through a learning link that is not easy for us, remembering becomes a struggle.

How You Can Benefit from Knowing Your Best Memory Superlink Learning Style and Brain Style: Improving to read: Improving Your Study and Test Taking Skills, and Increasing Test Scores

By discovering your best superlink memory learning style and brain style, you will know how to improve memory, reading comprehension, gain the ability to learn quickly, have strategies to study better, and increase your test scores. You will comprehend reading material better and improve your memory, making your study time more productive. Those who have used these techniques have drastically improved their scores on tests—whether for school tests, state or high stakes reading tests, entrance examinations such as the ACT, SAT, High School Placement Test, college boards, certification exams, or qualifying tests for a job or career.

Improving Your Communication and Relationships Issues and Problems with Others

Not only can you remember faster, you will learn how others' superlinks memory learning styles work, making you a better communicator, trainer, and instructor when you work with, train, or teach others. Do you have relationship issues and problems with others and want relationship advice? You can improve communication with those with whom you live or with whom you are in a relationship. Have you ever been frustrated because you spent an hour trying to give your child homework help and he or she still did not remember it? Knowledge of the eight memory superlinks gets your message across effectively. Whether you work in an office, a corporation, a factory, a store, or anywhere else, by identifying others' memory learning links you will be able to communicate more effectively with your boss, coworkers, employees, and customers, and improve relationships with them. You will find a new power to get your message across in a way that others can understand.

It has helped instructors train others in academic and nonacademic subjects such as learning a job, an art, a hobby, or a sport. For example, instructors at the Michael Jordan Golf Company, Director of Instruction and 1993 PGA Teacher of the Year, Charlie Long, and Golf Instructor and Missouri State Amateur Gold Champion, Maria Long, have said, "We have utilized learning styles while giving golf instruction for several years now. As teachers, it was a major source of frustration to give out what we knew was good information, only to see widely varied results with our learners. What we originally passed off as greater or lesser degrees of talent in our students we now recognize was due to the fact that we did not always give the information in our students' best way of receiving it. We now adapt our approach to the learners—a gold lesson can be a lengthy video viewing session; a richly detailed conversation; a hands-on walk through a new motion; or just a super-visual coaching session with short do instructions. We have greater peace of mind, and our students obviously love their progress. We feel that adapting to the student's learning style is maybe the real future of golf instruction. We know more than enough ways to swing—we just need better ways to help others understand." Their appreciation to the future of golf instruction holds equally true for instruction in all fields.

Small differences in communication due to various memory learning styles can stress even the closest relationship. Understanding how you and other individuals learn and remember best can also greatly improve your personal relationships and communication with the significant others in your life.

How to Use This Book

This book, *How to Improve Memory Quickly by Knowing Your Personal Memory Style: Quick, Easy Tips to Improve Memory through the Brain's Fastest Superlinks Memory and Learning Style,* is like eight books in one—a book for each of the eight superlinks memory learning styles and brain styles. You can read the whole book cover to cover, in order, or read only those sections that relate to your memory superlink, skipping the descriptions and strategies that do not relate to you. After you understand how to improve memory through your own memory superlink you may want to go back and read through the book again to learn about how people with other superlinks remember.

Note: If you do not know you or your family's and friend's superlink memory learning style and brain style you can either read through the descriptions in this book to see which

14

memory style(s) describe you, or you may wish to take a learning style inventory test or take the Superlinks to Accelerated Learning™ learning style and brain style inventory test before, while, or after reading the book. You can find instructions in the special Bonus for Readers section in the back of this book, *How to Improve Memory Quickly by Knowing Your Personal Memory Style: Quick, Easy Tips to Improve Memory through the Brain's Fastest Superlinks Memory and Learning Style*, on how to get to the website to take the online learning style inventory test which is instantly scored with your personalized report.

Have fun mastering techniques to improve rapidly increase memory!

CHAPTER 2:

FIND YOUR FASTEST WAY TO IMPROVE YOUR MEMORY QUICKLY USING BRAIN-BASED STRATEGIES

You *can* learn how to remember any subject quickly. You can increase your memory of whatever you read or learn by knowing your brain's fastest way of remembering. Whether you need to remember material for study skills, note taking, or test-taking skills for a test, learn and remember new skills on the job, or want to remember what you read, these revolutionary techniques can improve your comprehension and memory.

Many people worry that their current ability to remember is fixed and cannot be improved. Others worry about memory loss as one ages. However, take heart!

Medical breakthroughs have revealed the brain's power of plasticity. Molded by experiences in the past, the brain is also capable of establishing new pathways for learning and remembering. This exciting revolutionary discovery about brain plasticity means that we can change the way we remember, think, and learn. We are no longer restricted to limitations that have formed us so far; we can shape our future.

For over thirty years I have witnessed the astounding successes people have enjoyed using these revolutionary brain-based memory strategies I developed and applied based on research on how the brain learns and remembers. I am excited to share with readers in this book these easy-to-use techniques for remembering anything quickly. One of the approaches I developed, Virtual Reality Reading™, as part of the Superlinks to Accelerated Learning™ and Keys to Reading Success™ reading comprehension program, is based on research that when people inwardly experience in their brain what they are reading, using their fastest way of learning, their brain remembers it as well as if it were actually experienced outwardly. Our brain not only remembers better, but new, more effective patterns of learning, reading comprehension, and memory are set up in the brain to ensure mastery of any subject. The brain's ability to form new neural pathways, based on these accelerated learning and memory techniques, can alter and improve one's mental performance and retention.

An exciting breakthrough scientifically confirms the mechanism by which the Virtual Reality Reading comprehension and memory technique has worked.

Science has advanced so that the mechanism by which the brain learns could be demonstrated through medical scanning techniques. With the development of more precise scanning equipment such PET scans (positive emission tomography), Functional MRIs (functional Magnetic Resonance Imaging), and TMS (transcranial magnetic stimulation) used in experimental studies, evidence has surfaced that shows that by thinking about a task, new pathways in the brain develop as if someone had actually physically performed the task.

For example, Alvaro Pascual-Leone, a neuroscientist at Harvard Medical School, performed an experiment in which one group of people practiced a piano exercise using five fingers for two hours a day for five days. Each day, they took a TMS test in which a coil of wire held above their head sent a short magnetic pulse into the motor cortex of their brain. This allowed the scientist to observe the activity of neurons or nerve cells in that part of the brain. The TMS test helped the researchers map how much of the motor cortex controlled the finger movements to play the piano. After observing the results for five days, the scientists discovered that the part of the motor cortex used for these finger exercises on the piano spread to surrounding areas of the motor cortex. This revealed that extended connections were being made as the participants continued to practice the piano. That result was expected. Practicing playing the piano stimulated neurons that increased connections in the brain and expanded the amount of brain space devoted to that task. What was fascinating to the scientists though, and which bears out the Virtual Reality Reading™ comprehension and memory improvement technique, was what happened to the second group of people involved in the experiment.

The second group was asked to only *think* about playing the same five-finger piano exercise for two hours a day, for five days a week, without actually playing the piano. Neuron activity in the motor cortex also was measured by the TMS test. The scientists then compared the group that played the piano and the group that only imagined themselves playing the piano. The astounding results revealed that the group that imagined themselves playing the piano showed the same expansion of neuron activity in the region of the motor cortex as did those who actually played the instrument. Pascual-Leone later wrote, Mental practice resulted in a similar reorganization of the brain (from How the Brain Rewires Itself, *Time Magazine*, Jan. 19, 2007, by Sharon Begley). This experiment shows the power of mental training to change brain connections. This news is exciting because the general principles that I had discovered about learning and memory through research and application over thirty years was being proven through advanced instrumentation such as the TMS test.

This revolutionary Virtual Reality Reading™ comprehension and memory improvement technique forms one part of accelerated learning. The power of thought can form neural connections in the brain as if one physically performed a task. We know that most people can tell you what they did this morning or what they did yesterday. They can recall events in which they physically participated. The Virtual Reality Reading™ comprehension and memory improvement strategies translate what is read into visualization of the material as if one were participating, so that one can establish brain connections as if one had done the activity. The enhanced brain connections that are formed can more easily be stored and retrieved as memories and thus help the learner recall more information.

The next discovery supporting the Virtual Reality Reading™ comprehension and memory improvement program is that we all do not remember in the same way.

People of all ages, all genders, all walks of life, all cultures, and all nationalities have taken the two learning style inventory and brain style tests I developed: Superlinks to Accelerated Learning™ test, which contains the Linksman Learning Style Preference Assessment™ test and the Linksman Brain Hemispheric Preference Assessment™ test. The results reveal that people comprehend, remember, and learn in different ways. Their fastest way of learning and remembering is connected to how they take in, comprehend, and remember information from the world around them into their brain. Through a combination of nature and nurture, (genetics mingled with stimulation from the senses to the brain through life experiences), our brain takes in information differently. These experiences have established neural networks that are familiar, comfortable, and automatic in each of us. When we learn and remember through that pathway, we learn faster and more effectively and retain the information. Thus, when we know what our fastest pathway is and use techniques that are based on those pathways, we can learn faster and remember better.

By finding your fastest way of learning how to remember, you can increase reading comprehension, recall, and memory of any subject. People of all ages have found a dramatic difference in their ability to remember when they used their fastest memory superlink.

It is important to receive the right diagnosis of your best way of remembering. For the past thirty-five years, I have researched, developed, and field-tested what many educators consider to be the most accurate and comprehensive learning memory style and brain style assessment inventory test for determining one's fastest way of learning and remembering. To date, when anyone has taken this learning style memory preference test and altered their learning and memory techniques to their fastest way of remembering, they experienced a significant improvement in their ability to learn and remember. This has been more than anecdotal reporting. For example, I have applied this Superlinks to Accelerated Learning methodology to my learn-to-read program called Keys to Reading Success™. Through studies using the Keys to Reading Success™ reading comprehension and memory improvement program (which includes reading tests, reading practice, and memory strategies for kindergarten, grades one to twelve, college, and adult learners) measurements of reading test scores and reading performance in public schools (from elementary, middle, and high schools) revealed that from 88% to 99% of all students rose an average of two, three, four, and five years of growth in reading within months. This includes students who were in Regular Education programs as well as students in Special Education, Title I, Remedial Reading, At-risk, Gifted, and ELL (English language learners), ESL or ESOL (English as a Second Language), and Bi-lingual programs or those challenged by ADHD (Attention deficit hyperactivity disorder) or ADD (attention-deficit disorder). The other 1% or 2%, comprised mostly those in the categories of severe or profound mental retardation, who did not make gains of two or more grade levels in a few months, but did make gains of several months, which exceeded their previous performance without using their superlinks memory learning style. Since reading forms the basis of learning for a majority of subjects, improving and accelerating reading progress can make a significant difference in learning those subjects. The Keys to Reading Success™ reading comprehension and memory strategies help learners of all ages become top readers, able to comprehend and remember what one read for assignments in a course, a job, or a reading test in any content area subject. They are able to retain in long-term memory what one reads for mastery in any field. Thus, anyone who needs to learn a subject that requires remembering what one reads can dramatically improve his or her ability in that subject.

Thirty years of success stories document how people of all

ages have experienced a dramatic improvement in learning and memory based on the revolutionary techniques in this book. Superlinks brain- based memory strategies have helped people of all ages be successful. Here are a few case studies to illustrate the wide range of people it has helped:

Case Study 1: From Two Years of Not Reading a Single Word to Learning to Read in a Day

A first-grade boy from Virginia who had been left back in kindergarten for two years and was labeled as ADHD could not read a single word despite numerous attempts at school to teach him even first grade reading skills. His grandfather, a retired Navy pilot, observing the boy was bright, was puzzled as to why he could not learn to read. When his grandfather did some research on the Internet and discovered our revolutionary reading program based on accelerated reading comprehension and memory learning techniques, Keys to Reading Success™, he flew his grandson from Virginia to Naperville, Illinois, in the western suburbs of the Chicago area, to see if he could be helped. The Keys to Reading Success™ reading diagnostic test was given along with the Superlinks to Accelerated Learning™ learning style inventory tests. The reading diagnostic test confirmed that the boy could not read a single first grade reading level word and was, in fact, at a kindergarten level in reading, although he was the age of a second-grade student. The Superlinks learning style and brain style inventory tests showed that he was a kinesthetic right-brain learner who remembered best what he did kinesthetically. After the boy spent only two hours in a reading session using a kinesthetic right-brain learning reading comprehension, phonics, and memory technique, he was able to read a list of first grade words and the first pages of a book fluently by himself for the first time in his life and comprehend it. The boy was beaming, and the grandfather shed tears of joy. They continued the technique for a period of two weeks and the boy was able to read an entire sixty-page book consisting of full page stories at a first-grade reading level. Excited at finally being able to read, the boy clutched the book to his chest with pride, asking whoever passed him by whether they wanted to listen to him read aloud! Within months he was reading at a first-grade reading level and had renewed confidence and self-esteem that he was not stupid after all. He was taken off ADHD medication as it was medically confirmed that his reading problem was not due to having an attention-deficit hyperactive disorder but was merely a result of his being a kinesthetic right-brain learner who only needed the correct techniques for his unique way of learning and remembering to teach him how to learn to read.

Case Study 2: Never Too Old to Learn to Read

A baby-boomer gentleman in his fifties, who spent his whole life believing he could not read, decided that he wanted to give it one last chance—he wanted to be able to learn to read a book. When his Superlink memory learning and brain style, or fastest way of learning and remembering, was discovered, and the correct reading comprehension and memory techniques were used, he was also able to read successfully, opening new doorways for his life. He later said, I wish I had discovered this reading comprehension and memory technique as a child, as it would have dramatically changed the course of my life.

Case Study 3: The School District that No One Thought Could Raise Reading Test Scores

An entire school district in an area of low economic income, southwest of Chicago, near Joliet, Illinois, had not been meeting state standards in their state reading tests for six consecutive years and was on the state warning list, or probation. Lack of academic success had spiraled into a school with severe discipline problems, lack of motivation, and a cynicism towards any new reading program ever working since none had worked so far. Students in the entire school district went through a Keys to Reading Success™ reading diagnostic test and a Superlinks test of learning styles and brain hemispheric preference. Accelerated learning and memory techniques in reading (reading comprehension, memory improvement, phonics, fluency, vocabulary, note taking, study skills, and test-taking skills for the Illinois ISAT state reading tests) were used with the students to match each of their fastest way of learning.

Within six months, the students raised their reading levels on average growth of two to five years above their grade level, and for the first time they met state standards in reading on their state reading test. Discipline problems dropped to the point where the in-school suspension officer, who was used to numerous discipline referrals a day, said, "Now I am lonely as I hardly get any discipline referrals in my office. Students are engaged and excited about learning for the first time, and their discipline has improved."

Case Study 4: A School with 83% Non-English Speaking Students that Rose to Third Highest Reading Scores in the District in One Year

An elementary school in which 83% of the student population spoke Spanish as their primary language and were learning English as a second language had not yet met state reading standards as tested on the Illinois ISAT reading test. By finding each student's superlink learning style and brain style, or fastest way of learning, and then using the Keys to Reading Success™ reading comprehension and memory program to teach them to read fluently and remember vocabulary in English, including all the phonics and decoding patterns, in their unique learning memory and brain styles, they met state standards in reading and came in third highest in the East Aurora school district.

Case Study 5: From Failure to Success in One Year in an East Los Angeles, California, Charter School

A charter school in East Los Angeles, California, was opened to focus on Afro-American culture (CLAS, an acronym for the Culture and Language Academy of Success) as it attempted to raise student reading achievement. The parents, wanting to see improved educational opportunities for their children, received permission from the Los Angeles Unified School District to form a charter school. At first, the students had not met state reading standards, but after adopting the revolutionary accelerated learning and memory techniques in the Keys to Reading Success™ reading comprehension and memory improvement program and its Superlinks to Accelerated Learning™ learning and memory style and brain style inventory tests, the charter school met the California state reading standards within one school year. Using the brain-based methods of accelerated learning and memory based on Superlinks™ and Keys to Reading Success™, their dedicated teaching staff was trained in these methods, and within less than one school year, the elementary school improved their reading test scores and showed the highest growth in reading scores in the entire Los Angeles Unified School District.

Case Study 6: ACT Reading Test Scores Improved Dramatically in Months

Students who had scored in the low teens on their reading ACT test (college entrance exams) improved their reading test scores to the high twenties and into the thirties in a matter of months using reading comprehension, memory, study skills, and test-taking techniques that matched their fastest way of learning and remembering, enabling them to score high enough to be accepted into college.

Case Study 7: Raising Preschoolers and Kindergarteners Reading Levels to Become Top First Grade Readers and Place in Advanced, Gifted, and Enriched Programs

In a school in a high minority and high poverty area, reading scores had been so low that the community, the parents, and even the teachers believed it hopeless that any of the student could ever learn. However, using accelerated reading comprehension, phonics, fluency, and memory techniques that matched their superlinks memory and learning and brain styles, preschoolers and kindergarteners were able to learn how to read at a first and second reading grade level within less than a year so that when they entered first grade, they were at the top of their class in reading. This progress continued and as they entered second grade and third grade and higher, many ended up qualifying for advanced, gifted and talented, and enrichment programs. Their reading levels improved to between two and eight years *above* their age. In fact, ten of them who were previously thought to be unable to learn were placed into a gifted program at a gifted and talented magnet school. When the teachers realized how these new reading and memory techniques they were trained to use had produced such startling results by the end of the school year, some had tears come to their eyes to see that their students were not dumb or stupid after all. They only needed the key to their brains so they could learn in their best way of learning and remembering. Many teachers felt renewed passion for teaching when they saw that it was not hopeless and they could make a difference in the lives of their students once they knew how.

Case Study 8: A Losing University Football Team Has Its First Winning Season through Superlinks Reading Comprehension and Memory Strategies

A university football team that never had a winning season tested all the athletes for their superlink learning and brain styles. The athletic coaches were trained in using each player's superlink memory, learning, and brain styles to teach the football playbook. After altering the football coaches' teaching styles to match each of the player's superlink memory and learning style, the football team had their first winning season! Applying these techniques to academic subjects, they were also able to improve reading test scores to do better in their content subject area classes.

Case Study 9: College Students, Medical School Students, Professionals in all Fields, and Athletes Helped through Brain-based Accelerated Memory and Learning Methods

Medical students have been able to raise their scores on their medical examinations using these revolutionary methods. Professionals in all fields, including business, law, finances, technology, medicine, and real estate, have been able to improve their on-the- job performance and improve on certification examinations using the Superlink accelerated learning, reading comprehension, and memory techniques.

Athletes and coaches have used these memory techniques to improve sports performance in areas such as football and golf.

Write Your Own Success Story

Techniques in this book can also help you identify your fastest way of remembering and learning so you can write your own success story. Once you know your own brain's secrets, you too can use it to improve reading comprehension, memory, note taking, study skills, and test taking skills to learn anything quickly.

You are invited to share your success stories by sending them in if you want to share them to give hope to others who may be frustrated or struggling with memory as you once did!

CHAPTER 3:

DIFFERENCES IN HOW PEOPLE WITH DIFFERENT LEARNING STYLES REMEMBER INFORMATION FROM THE WORLD AROUND THEM

Why do we have a preference for one mode of remembering over another? It is all about the technology of the brain. What form of stimulation did we receive more of as we were growing up? Did our caretakers give us many objects, pictures, mobiles, or illustrated books at which to look? Was there much talking, conversation, dialogue, or music in our childhood? Maybe we were given a great amount of hands-on activities to do like finger-painting, stringing beads, coloring, board games, or toys that required the use of our hands and fingers.

Were we encouraged to be more actively engaged in running, jumping, crawling, swimming, playing ball, building with blocks, making play-houses, or doing competitive activities? Whatever stimulation we received, our brains were grooving memory pathways along those lines. Over time, those networks of sensory pathways became more firmly established and more automatic. When something is automatic we do not have to think about it—it comes easily. Thus, we feel more comfortable and learn how to remember faster when working through that modality.

Over thirty years of interviewing and assessing the memory and learning style and brain style preferences of people from all walks of life, there are certain patterns of behavior, thought, comprehension, and memory that identify

31

those who have one sensory preference over another. Let us take the scenario of a person entering a room. The experience is different for people who have a different memory and learning style preference. The information that comes in, how the person comprehends the experience, and how he or she remembers it is different for people of various learning and memory styles. Of course, there are people who learn through a combination of two or more learning and memory styles and some who use all of them! Depending upon the preference, or the combination, that room provides a different experience for each of them.

How a Visual Learner Remembers Input from the World

If a growing child has received more stimulation through the pathways involving seeing, then that person relies more on that sense when taking in, comprehending, and remembering stimulation from the world. When this person enters a room, what is most noticed and remembered are the visuals—the color of the room, the paintings hanging on the walls, the size and shape of the furniture, printed material such as magazines or newspapers, and what people look like.

They may notice or recall anything that is out of order or not matching color-wise. They are attuned visually to the room. When they think about, comprehend, and remember their experience, they focus on what they were seeing. When they have to remember the room, they remember best what they saw. Over time, they identify themselves as a visual learner who remembers visually.

How an Auditory Learner Remembers Input from the World

If a child grows up exposed to much conversation and dialogue or music and sounds, then the pathways for remembering auditory input is more developed. Thus, when this person enters a room, the auditory stimulus is most noticed and recalled. This person will notice and remember the sounds in the room, such as talking, dialogue, conversation, the noise of passing cars, the whirl of a fan or hum of a computer, or a cell phone ringing in another room. This person will notice and recall best what people are saying and the sound of their voices. Thus, when they think about, comprehend, or remember their experience in the room, they focus on what sounds they were hearing or what people were saying. When they have to remember the room, they remember best what they heard. Thus, they develop a preference for being an auditory learner who remembers best auditorially.

How a Tactile Learner Remembers Input from the World

If a child has been exposed to activity involving using the hands or fingers, or there is a lot of stimulus on the skin, such as variations in heat and cold, softness and hardness, roughness and smoothness, pleasant or unpleasant sensations, or a lot of intensity of feelings either verbally expressed or nonverbally communicated, then the tactile modality and memory has received more stimulation in the brain's neural pathways. When such a person enters a room, he or she notices and recalls the nonverbal communication as expressed

33

through people's body language, facial expressions, or tones of voice, plus the feelings they get from others or from the room itself. This person will focus on and remember what can be touched or felt, or what the hands can do in the room, such as feeling a soft couch, writing, picking up objects to hold, and any other hands-on activity. This person will focus on hands-on experiences or the feelings they got from the room or from people. When remembering the experience, this person will remember best what was felt and what was touched using the hands. Therefore, they develop a preference for being a tactile learner or remembering tactilely.

How a Kinesthetic Learner Remembers Input from the World

If a child has had much stimulation through movement of his or her body and large muscles, then that pathway becomes more comfortable for that learner.

When this person enters a room, the first question that arises is, what can I do here? This person looks for space to move around, physical activities that can be done, and some challenge by which a goal can be achieved or won. When processing and remembering the experience, this person focuses on the action in the room. When trying to remember the room, this person best remembers what he or she did in the room. They then develop a preference for being a kinesthetic learner, remembering kinesthetically.

Learning and Memory Style Alone is Only Part of the Process

Besides remembering through our fastest learning and memory style, the information is further processed in the brain. Some people process and remember things in a sequential or step-by-step order. Others process and remember information by getting the big picture or main idea first and then fitting in the details. Medical researchers have previously identified sequential thinking processes take place in the left side of the brain, and the global overview thinking processes happen in the right side of the brain. Whether one subscribes to that distinction or not, or as brain research identifies exactly where they take place, for the purposes of defining the two types of processing and remembering, sequential thinking is referred to in this book as left brain, while global thinking is referred to as right brain. Whether science later proves sequential thought is somewhere else does not matter so much as knowing that we want to learn and remember new things sequentially as opposed to learning and remembering new things through a global overview that does not focus on steps in order. The memory technique that matches how we learn and recall is what matters most when we are learning and remembering, no matter what terms are used for them, or where they are actually taking place in the brain.

Similarly, besides the order in which we process and remember information, we also process and recall through words or images. Some people think and remember more in words. They talk to themselves and think about what is happening through language. Some people think and remember more in terms of pictures.

They recall images, colors, shapes, designs, faces, and patterns and remember these the best. Some remember equally through both. Again, whether words vs. graphics or pictures are actually localized in one part of the brain is not as important as knowing that is how we recall information faster. For the sake and ease of terminology, in this book, in recognition that brain science is identifying multiple areas of the brain in which various processes take place, remembering through words will be referred to as left-brain functioning; and remembering through images or pictures will be referred to as right-brain functioning. Knowing whether we need text or pictures when we remember can help us accelerate our comprehension, memory, and mastery of a subject, irrespective of the parts of the brain such functions are actually taking place.

Your Superlink is the Combination of Your Memory Learning Style and Brain Hemispheric Preference

In the early 1970s, work was done regarding learning styles. In those days, people were classified as one of three styles: visual, auditory, and kinesthetic.

Later, the term tactile was lumped in with kinesthetic, keeping the classification as three styles. In over thirty years of work, I was one of the few who recognized that a tactile learner is extremely different from a kinesthetic learner. Tactile and kinesthetic learners are two distinct types of learners and have different learning needs. Thus, I separate learning styles into four categories. In the early 1980s, as I used learning style teaching methods and memory techniques to teach people, I also observed repeatedly that visual learners were not all the same. I realize that some visual learners focused on printed words in text, while others focused on pictures, images, and graphics.

This same phenomenon occurred with auditory learners. Some auditory learners were great at memorizing lectures, while other auditory learners could not repeat a word of a lecture in a university hall if their life depended on it. Yet, they may have been highly aware of sounds, music, and sound effects.

I also realized that not all tactile learners were alike. Some focused on writing words, while others were not good at writing but excelled in drawing or making hands-on projects. Some were able to express their feelings in words, while others expressed their feelings through nonverbal communication.

Finally, not all kinesthetic people were alike.

Some liked to learn by verbal instructions, and others got annoyed when anyone spoke when they were engaged in activity. They preferred instead nonverbal demonstration that they could copy. Some kinesthetic people liked to talk about what they did, while others did not want to talk at all about the physical experiences in which they engaged.

Through these observations, I discovered that some visual learners were left-brain thinkers, while other visual learners were right-brain thinkers. There were visual left-brain learners who learned faster and remembered better by seeing text; and there were visual right brain learners who learned faster and remembered better by seeing pictures or graphics. The same was true of the other learning and memory styles. I saw dramatic increases in learning speed and recall when the learning style and brain hemispheric preference memory techniques were combined. I thus coined the term superlink to describe the combination of one's learning style and brain hemispheric preference to remember best. I thus named the strategies as the Superlinks to Accelerated Learning™. Since the 1980s, I have tracked the use of Superlinks in the teaching of reading with entire bodies of students in schools, from elementary school, to middle school and high school, and to college students, and adults in various professions. Without fail, people were able to learn faster, remember better, and master any subject when taught in their superlink style—the combination of learning and memory style and brain hemispheric preference style.

This accelerated system of memory was so effective, I created an entire pre-K, kindergarten, grade one through grade twelve, and college and adult reading curriculum program based on this Superlinks to Accelerated Learning™ and named it Keys to Reading Success™. This method has been studied and researched and have proven time and again to raise reading levels of 88%-99% of all students in a school anywhere from two, three, four, or five grade reading levels— on average— within months. The longest time for these gains to take place has been six to eight months, and has occurred as rapidly as two to four months' time. This includes students who are in Regular Education, Gifted, Special Education, Title I, or Remedial Reading programs, students with ADHD and ADD, and students who need to learn English who are in ELL (English language learners), ESL or ESOL (English as a Second Language), or Bilingual or Dual Language programs. It works to improve reading levels in both males and female. It works for people of all cultures or language groups. It works for people of all ages, from the very young to adults who have retired. Using the Superlinks to Accelerated Learning™

technique with the Keys to Reading Success™ reading comprehension and memory improvement program has helped students become top readers, to comprehend what they read, to remember what was read for an assignment or test, and to retain in long-term memory what was read for mastery in any field.

For this reason, it is recommended that one take both the Superlinks Learning Style Preference Assessment™ tests and the Brain Hemispheric Preference Assessment™ inventory tests for the most complete and comprehension diagnosis of one's best and fastest way of learning and remembering.

Knowing Your Learning and Memory Style Can Speed Up Your Learning

As our brain takes in the world through the filter of our learning style, or combination of styles, that network of thinking is easier to use for comprehending, learning, and remembering. In our unique learning and memory style, we take in information faster, focus on comprehending and thinking about what we learned, and recall and memorize the material better. These variations in strategies can help us learn how to learn and recall any subject faster. If we know our own unique way of learning and remembering, we can use that information to help us remember any subject more rapidly. It will open doors for us to remember more and learn more quickly. Knowing the keys to our own brain's memory can help us ask for what we need from an instructor, and if not provided by that teacher, help us provide for ourselves the strategy to master any subject. If the learning environment in which we find ourselves does not match the way we remember faster, we will have some strategies to use by ourselves to translate any subject into the way we need to recall it so we are independent and can learn and remember, even on our own.

I developed what I named the Virtual Reality Reading™ comprehension and memory improvement strategies to help you take in information that you read in your best and fastest way of remembering. Once you know this technique, it forms the basis of many other comprehension tasks, study skills, memory skills, and test-taking skills. You can use this virtual reality reading comprehension and memory technique to effectively learn and recall anything quickly.

Beyond this technique, there are many other skills and teaching methods needed to master any subject. Building on the virtual reality comprehension and memory techniques is a series of skills. These are all designed to increase comprehension and memory of whatever one is learning.

PART 2:
FIND YOUR SUPERLINK
IMPROVING YOUR MEMORY QUICKLY

CHAPTER 4:
FIND YOUR SUPERLINKS MEMORY STYLE PREFERENCE AND BRAIN HEMISPHERIC PREFERENCE

How to Take the Superlinks Linksman Learning Style Preference Assessment™ and Linksman Brain Hemispheric Preference Assessment™ Inventory Tests

Over the years, thousands of people have requested that I score the test for them, to ensure accuracy and save them time. To save even further time and make it easy for people, I spent five years converting it into an online assessment test that people could easily take using the computer, so the program could be instantly scored and provide detailed complete and instant results. The online test is now available in three places: at www.readinginstruction.com or at www.superlinkslearning.com or at www.keystoreadingsuccess.com, an accelerated reading program for grades pre-kindergarten, Grade One through Grade Twelve, college, and adult reading. The test is the same whether taken in any of these three websites. Keys to Reading Success™, is a pre-K, kindergarten, Grade 1 through Grade 12, college, and adult reading program to teach both how to learn to read and how to improve in memory and reading. It includes reading and listening comprehension, memory, phonics, fluency, vocabulary, phonemic awareness, study skills, note taking, and test-taking skills in reading and in any content area subject. Once you take the online learning style and brain style inventory learning profile tests, you will get your instantly-scored personalized results with a detailed report on how you remember the best, what materials you need, what is the best learning environment, what are the best learning and memory tips and strategies, and how you best communicate with others and want others to communicate with you.

When you take the Superlinks online assessment tests to determine your learning and memory style and brain style, it is highly recommended that you answer the questions as accurately as possible. If you do not answer these accurately and the results indicate that you have a different learning and memory style or brain hemispheric preference than what you really prefer, then you will not be learning and remembering in your most effective way. For each Superlinks learning and memory style and brain style, there are different methods to use, and it would be ineffective for you to use the wrong technique. So, be as accurate as you can—as painful as it may be for some!

The key to answering the questions is to select the answers or choices that are most natural or comfortable for you. Although we may be able to make ourselves to behave in ways described in the other choices—and we often have to do that on the job or in other situations—one choice will probably feel best for us if left to our own devices. Just as we can force ourselves to write with our nondominant hand, we may also force ourselves to behave in two, three, or four different ways (described in each question) depending on the circumstance. The question to ask yourself is, Which way feels the best and is the least stressful? It is in that spirit that you should respond to the questions.

What happens if you truly feel you can select more than one choice? It may be that for some of the questions, you absolutely know that two or three choices (and some people, even all the choices) are equally true of you. In that case, go ahead and select all those that equally describe you. First try to settle on one choice, and if you sure that there is more than one best answer, then select the others also.

When you have completed taking the *Linksman Learning Style Preference Assessment*™ test, next take the *Brain Hemispheric Preference Assessment*™ test to determine your preference for which of the functions of the two hemispheres of the brain you use for understanding the stimuli you receive from the world and for remembering and storing the information. Just as you did in the learning style preference assessment, you will be selecting the best of two choices that is the most natural, comfortable, and stress-free for you.

If you absolutely feel that both choices are really you, then select both. That too is a brain hemispheric preference style. Make sure you do not choose both to take the easy way out and to rush through the assessment test. If you have to choose both answers, do it because you have given it full consideration and know for certain that both describe you equally well.

After taking the *Learning Style Preference Assessment*™ and the *Brain Hemispheric Preference Assessment*™ tests, the results are automatically scored to find your best memory superlink.

Since the 1980s, when I began using learning and memory styles and brain hemispheric preferences, I realized there was a difference between those who were visual learners with a right-brain preference and those who were visuals with a left-brain preference. Similarly, there were auditory learners with a right-brain preference and some with a left- brain preference, and the way these two groups learned and remembered differed vastly.

While teachers who used learning styles would only assess whether their students were visual, auditory, tactile, or kinesthetic, and those who assessed brain hemispheric preference would only concentrate on the differences between the right and left sides of the brain, I had not found any system that combined the two. For years, I always looked at the whole picture—learning and memory style and brain hemispheric preference combined. Working closely with a large range of learners, I saw in case after case that both assessments had to be taken into account in order to accelerate one's learning. Thus, I found there were eight broad categories and a vast difference between the way each group learned and remembered. I have named these categories the eight superlinks to accelerated memory and learning because they provide the fastest and most effective link between the material to be learned and recalled and our brain. The word *superlink* is used to make a distinction between the use of this method of combing both brain style and learning and memory style and the use of the method of only evaluating visual, auditory, tactile, or kinesthetic learning and memory styles without considering brain style preferences. Since the term *learning style* as used by most people excludes brain hemispheric preference, I have coined the term *superlink* because that includes both our learning and memory style preference and our brain hemispheric preference.

After taking both assessment tests, the *Learning Style Preference Assessment* and the *Linksman Brain Hemispheric Preference Assessment,* you will know your own superlink to remembering and learning. Here are the possible main combinations, but you can be a combination of two or more of these as well:

- Visual Left-Brain
- Visual Right-Brain
- Auditory Left-Brain
- Auditory Right-Brain
- Tactile Left-Brain
- Tactile Right-Brain
- Kinesthetic Left-Brain
- Kinesthetic Right-Brain

These are the eight superlinks to accelerated learning and memory.

Superlinks Combinations

There are people who may use a combination of these eight superlinks. If your brain hemispheric preference is integrated, your possible Superlinks are:

- Visual Right and Left-Brain Integrated
- Auditory Right and Left-Brain Integrated
- Tactile Right and Left-Brain Integrated
- Kinesthetic Right and Left-Brain Integrated

The possible combinations of superlinks for mixed preferences are:

- Visual Right and Left-Brain Mixed Preference
- Auditory Right and Left-Brain Mixed Preference
- Tactile Right and Left-Brain Mixed Preference
- Kinesthetic Right and Left-Brain Mixed Preference

You may also be a combination of memory and learning styles. Some people can be visual and auditory; others can be tactile and auditory. Some use two, three, or all four learning and memory styles equally; others may use all four learning and memory styles and have an integrated preference for both sides of the brain—this person would be equally using all brain modalities at once.

The following chapters contain descriptions of each type of learner and ways to use these keys to learn how to remember anything quickly. You will understand what each learning and memory style preference and each brain hemispheric preference means for you, and how the combination of the two—your superlink to accelerated learning and remembering—can help you learn better, faster, and more easily, and retain and remember better.

Suggested Note to Readers: If you plan on taking the Superlinks *Learning Style Preference Assessment*™ and the *Brain Hemispheric Preference Assessment*™ tests, you may want to consider doing so before reading the descriptions in the rest of the book. Why? If you know the descriptions of each, some people may be predisposed to gear their answers on the assessment towards picking choices they believe will lead to their results showing them to be a particular learning and memory style and brain style, because they want to be that style, or think they are, rather than letting the results come from their unbiased choices. I have seen some cases over the years where people wanted to be identified with one particular style, and if they knew the characteristics, picked choices on the assessment that would lead their results to turn out that way. The value in taking it before knowing the specific characteristics is that it allows you to focus on each question and the choices that truly describe you, so that you see the results of your unbiased answers. However, if you prefer to read the descriptions first, and then take the assessment, you can do so if you can answer the questions by selecting choices that describe you and not what you wish to be or what you think others want you to be.

If you wish to take the online test, go to: www.readinginstruction.com and select Superlinks Assessment. As a reader of this book, *How to Improve Memory Quickly by Knowing Your Personal Memory Style: Quick, Easy Tips to Improve Memory through the Brain's Fastest Superlinks Memory and Learning Style*, enter the special gift discount code HTLAQ for a special reduced rate for the on-line Superlinks test. If you are a teacher, coach, trainer, employer, or someone who wishes to have students, trainees, employees, athletes, or group members take the test, you can get bulk licenses at special rates by contacting: info@keyslearning.com or go to www.keystoreadingsuccess.com or visit www.superlinkslearning.com.

If you are reading this book to know about the different learners to help you be a better teacher, trainer, sports coach, trainer of trainers, instructor, parent, life coach, psychologist, psychiatrist, or medical doctor who deals with educational or learning and memory issues of your patients, or you are an employer who wants to learn how to train your employees to improve in remembering what they are taught for doing their jobs, or you wish to improve your own memory, reading comprehension, communication, study skills, note taking, or test-taking skills and do not wish to take the assessment, you can proceed to read the rest of the book for your own specific purposes and goals.

PART 3:
WHAT DOES MEMORY STYLE PREFERENCE AND BRAIN HEMISPHERIC PREFERENCE MEAN TO IMPROVE MEMORY QUICKLY?

CHAPTER 5:
WHAT IS A MEMORY LEARNING STYLE?

Our memory learning style is one part of our superlink to accelerated remembering. Research has identified that people remember in different ways. We rely on all our senses to receive information from the outside world, yet, over time, many people develop one sense more than others have done and find it easier to rely on that one for recalling new material. This is how we develop a preference for one type (or combination of several types) of memory style. If we want to remember something rapidly, the material needs to be presented to us in our most developed pathway to the brain— our memory style. There are four main memory style preferences: visual, auditory, tactile, and kinesthetic.

Visual learners remember best by seeing.

Auditory learners remember best by listening, hearing themselves talk, and discussing their thoughts with others.

Tactile learners remember best by touching or feeling sensation on their skin, by using their hands and fingers, and connecting what they learn to their sense of touch or to their feeling, either physically or emotionally.

Kinesthetic learners remember best by moving their large, or gross motor, muscles in space, through performing actions with their body, and by being actively involved in the learning process through simulations, role-playing, experimenting, exploration, and movement, and through participating in real-life activities.

Learners who use other senses: Though rare, there are some learners who rely on their sense of taste or smell. They can be identified because they have an acute sense of smell or taste, are sensitive to odors or tastes, and can remember well by involving these senses.

Memory Style and the Brain

Brain research has advanced enough so that we have a *limited* understanding of how the brain works. Although there is still much to learn, we do know some basic principles that are relevant to understanding how we remember. As our brains are exposed to stimuli, new interconnections between nerve cells are created. This quality is known as *brain plasticity*. The more stimuli we receive, the more interconnections and learning patterns are formed. Thus, as certain learning patterns become more rapid, easier, and automatic, we learn and remember more quickly, reinforcing the development of our best memory style. This is the essence of improving memory.

We have pathways between our senses and the brain. If over time we have relied more upon our eyes, then the passageways between the nerves in our eyes and the part of the brain that interprets visual stimulus developed more than passageways between the other senses and the brain. As a result, we find it easier to rely upon our eyes and are visual learners who recall best what we see. For some people, the neural connections between the ears and the part of the brain that interprets auditory stimulus is stronger; thus, they find it easier and quicker to learn through the ears and are auditory learners who recall best what they hear. For others, the neural passageways between the skin, hands, and fingers and the part of the brain that interprets tactile stimuli of feeling physical sensation and physiological responses to emotion has been used more and those people find it easier to learn though the sense of touch and are tactile learners who recall best tactilely. Some have made more use of their large motor muscles, so the neural pathways from their muscles to that part of the brain that senses body motion have become stronger and are kinesthetic learners who recall best what they do.

When learning and remembering something new, we need to concentrate on assimilating the new information, process, or skill. We do not want to be encumbered by trying to learn and remember through a weak sensory modality, so, to accelerate learning, new information should be presented in our best memory style. If you want to develop other memory styles, it is best to do so when you are not trying to learn and recall new material. The basic rule of thumb is: if you want to remember something quickly, recall it through your preferred memory style.

How Memory Styles Develop

Some of our tendencies are genetically inherited, some are a result of exposure to certain stimuli over a long period of time, and some develop due to one's reliance on that particular sense for survival. According to research on brain plasticity, these repeated stimuli strengthen certain passageways between one or more senses and the brain.

There are men and women who fall into each of the memory style categories. There are visual men and visual women. Similarly, there are auditory men and auditory women, tactile men and tactile women, and kinesthetic men and kinesthetic women. While certain memory styles—such as kinesthetic, movement-oriented style—seems to be attributed in some societies erroneously more to men, while others, such as the tactile memory style in some circles seem to be erroneously attributed more to women, these stereotypes do not hold true in reality. In the past, cultural pressures may have exerted influence on members of each gender to exhibit certain behaviors, and succumbing to this pressure, over time, some members of each gender habitually began to act a certain way. Through this repetition and the brain's power of plasticity, new neural patterns were charted that developed into a stronger preference for a particular memory style. Alternatively, some people may feel it is culturally acceptable to answer a question in a certain way as they feel that is the way a member of that gender should act, but it is not really the way that an individual thinks, recalls, and processes information in his or her brain. This underscores the importance of people who take a learning and memory style or brain style assessment test to answer as truthfully and closely as possible as to which choice describes them the best and not what they believed others want them to say. More recently, as people of both genders are given more opportunities to engage in a wider range of experiences not limited by gender stereotypes, they will develop more along the lines of their natural way of learning and remembering, resulting in people of both sexes developing strengths in any of the learning and memory styles and brain styles. With people being more informed about learning and memory styles and brain styles, it is hoped that parents and teachers will realize the importance of exposing the young to stimuli that develop all their senses, giving them an opportunity to develop their *whole* brain and make better use of their natural talents.

A question frequently raised is: Since traditional schools teach people mostly through the visual and auditory sense, wouldn't all learners develop into visual and auditory learners? The answer can best be understood by a similar question: If you are right-handed, wouldn't you become left-handed if you were forced to use only the left hand in school? Think of what that would be like. You could *force* yourself to use the left hand but you would be slower, more conscious of the motions of writing than to doing the actual work, and it might take you years to become as proficient with your left hand as you are with your right hand. (The same situation would be applicable if you were to make left-handed people write with their right hand.) It may take you the same number of years to develop your non-dominant hand as it took to become automatic with your dominant hand, putting you several years back in development of skills that require writing ability.

Similarly, if you were a visual, tactile, or kinesthetic learner, you could force yourself to develop your auditory learning and memory style, but during the years you were developing it you would struggle with material presented auditorially, putting you at a disadvantage in that environment. The same holds true for forcing auditory,

57

tactile, or kinesthetic learners into a visual environment. When learning something new, you naturally want to use your most comfortable sense to accelerate progress. At other times, you can strengthen your weaker senses, and over time they will become stronger, but they will not equal your ability in your strongest sense unless you stop using it for a part of that time.

The Four Types of Memory Styles

While each learner is unique, people who have the same memory style share some similar characteristics. In the following chapters on the eight superlinks, each memory style will be described so you can understand yourself and others.

If you have already taken the Superlinks assessment test (see the back of the book for information on where to go to take it), you may want to begin with the chapter on your own superlink memory and learning style first, and then read descriptions of the other types. If you scored equally in several memory and learning styles, read each description of those two, three, or possibly four styles. Highlight the characteristics in each that describe your personal profile. You may also recognize qualities of other people you know.

You may find that most characteristics describe you, or only some. If the latter is true, then all the descriptions of one memory style alone may not match you completely because you use a mixture of two or more memory styles. It could be that in our jobs we develop other senses and were identifying with our work persona. If that is the case, you may find that you have several memory styles—your work style, your style when dealing with other people, and the style you are at heart. Although we may be strong in one memory style, this does not mean we neglect to use other styles in different situations. Thus, you will need to read the characteristics of each to see which portions in combination apply to you. Establishing the accurate combination is important, so when you get to the learning activities, strategies, and practice activities in the book, you employ the ones that match your combination of styles. The descriptions are not meant to be a system for labeling people for all times; rather, they allow us to form a profile of ourselves and help us communicate better and recall more easily and rapidly. The chapters on the eight Superlinks fully describe the combinations of memory and learning style plus brain hemispheric preference and its application to improve memory for us in reading, comprehension, study skills, note taking, and test-taking skills to remember any subject quickly.

CHAPTER 6:
WHAT IS A BRAIN HEMISPHERIC PREFERENCE?

The brain is divided into two hemispheres or halves—the right hemisphere and the left hemisphere. While we all use both sides of the brain, many people process and store information using functions on one side more than the other, exhibiting a *brain hemispheric preference*. A preference for one side of the brain develops when we use particular neural pathways more, developing them to a higher degree; we become more skilled in using that hemisphere. It is not that we are incapable of using the other side of the brain, but when we use one half more, over time it feels more comfortable and natural to use.

When people receive instruction in a way that does not match their brain hemispheric preference they may take longer to learn, they may struggle, or even fail. However, when we communicate in the way that matches our brain hemispheric preference, we learn and remember more easily and quickly.

Scientists have helped us understand some of the characteristics of the right and left sides of the brain.

Each side looks at life differently. Thus, someone who processes and remembers mostly through the right side of the brain will experience an event or situation differently from one who processes and remembers mostly through the left side of the brain.

Our brain hemispheric preference is not a conscious choice, but we may grow up using mostly one side for many tasks. As children, we may have been exposed to many linear tasks, so our brain had enough stimuli to develop neural pathways that support linear thinking, referred to as left-brain thinking. Or, we may have been exposed to many wholistic and global experiences, stimulating the development of global thinking, referred to as right brain thinking.

Neither side of the brain is superior to the other; they merely do different tasks important for survival.

Ideally, people should be able to use both sides of their brain equally well. Unfortunately, this information on brain hemispheric preference which has been known to researchers for decades has still not filtered down to everyone engaged in teaching and training, whether parents, teachers, instructors, sports or athletic coaches, trainers, or employers. Left to chance, some people might end up using one side more than the other and relying on that side for all tasks, even those more appropriately handled by the other side. This is the reason that many people have difficulty learning and remembering, or they find it takes them a long time to remember.

While waiting for educational systems to use these new memory methods that can train all students to engage both hemispheres of the brain, we need to find ways to deal with the struggles of students who have mostly developed one side of their brain through their life experiences yet are being taught through methods targeting their less developed or less preferred side of their brain. Thus, if you have favored one side of the brain for most tasks, in this book, *How to Improve Memory Quickly*, you will learn techniques to adapt any learning situation to be compatible with your brain's memory style preference.

Can we develop the other side of our brain if we have a preference? Yes, according to research into brain plasticity, we can, but it takes time, although the process is accelerated when learning through one's Superlinks memory and learning style and brain style. Everyone has had a certain number of years learning and remembering through one side of the brain, and you can calculate how long it may take to balance that by developing the other side. In the meantime, through your superlinks memory and learning style and brain style preference, you can use it to your advantage to improve memory by having material presented to you in a way that is compatible with the way your brain recalls. The rule is: learn and remember something new through your preferred side.

When not learning, develop the undeveloped side of the brain.

While scientists are still mapping the brain and have not yet completed work that will give us a fuller understanding of how the entire brain works, we know a great deal and can apply these findings to the field of improving memory.

Learning and Memory Style and Brain Hemispheric Preference

Learning and memory style relates to the different ways of inputting or receiving and recalling material from the world and conveying those messages from our senses to the brain. Brain hemispheric preference deals with what we do with the data—how we process or think about, comprehend, remember, and store it once information reaches the brain.

The sensory data from our eyes, ears, sense of touch, or the muscles of our body can be channeled to the right side or left side of the brain. Each side processes, remembers, and stores the information in different ways. It is essential to know these differences to learn how to improve memory quickly.

Some educators focus only on using learning styles when teaching, while others focus only on using brain hemispheric preference. To have a total picture of the way people need to learn, a blending of both is required; thus, the development of the concept of a superlink: learning and memory style *plus* brain hemispheric preference. It is more effective to know both our best learning and memory style and our brain hemispheric preference to improve our memory.

Differences between the Left and Right Hemispheres

Processing Information: Symbolically versus Sensorially

One difference in the way the sides of the brain process and remember is that the left side processes and recalls data symbolically in the form of letters, numbers, words, and abstract ideas, and the right side processes and recalls data in a sensory way, perceiving the world through the senses without words.

The left hemisphere allows human beings to have the gift of language. Without language, we would only perceive what we see, hear, taste, smell, and touch, and our movements, without words. We would not be able to talk about our experiences or communicate them to others. In most people, the left side of the brain handles language, although there are exceptions: One report states that in five percent of right-handed people and thirty percent of left-handed people, the speech area is in the right hemisphere of the brain. (From *The Brain: A Neuroscience Primer*, 2nd Edition, by Richard F.

Thompson. New York: W.H. Freeman and Co., 1993, p. 397).
Think of the hemisphere in which our speech and language center is located as a built-in translator that takes whatever happens and puts words or numbers to it.

The right side of the brain processes and recalls information without language. It perceives sensation of sight, touch, smell, taste, movement, and the sounds of the human voice, music, and nature without putting words or labels to the experience. It perceives life as a movie without words.

Although everyone processes language, the difference is that some people *first* process everything into words and language, while other people *first* perceive the event as a pure sensory experience without words. As the material is processed and recalled in your mind, you can think about it either in words, as if a dialogue were going on in your head, or you can think about it in sensory images full of sight, sound, smell, taste, and touch, as well as movement, without words. If you wonder how this is possible, think of a time when you saw someone you knew but could not remember his or her name. You tried so hard to remember but drew a blank—yet you were sure you knew the person. This is an example of how the right brain functions—without words.

This information is critical in terms of improving memory. Why? If someone processes information and recalls in symbols such as words, he or she will respond better to being taught in terms of words and language. If someone processes and recalls information in sensory images, he or she will respond better to being taught in terms of sensory images and experiences. When we match the presentation of new material to our brain hemispheric preference, remembering it is easier. When we do not do this, we may struggle with remembering new material or may not recall the material at all.

This does not mean none of us use both sides of the brain to process and recall information. All who have both sides of their brain intact, can process and recall words and sensory images, blending the two together to learn and perform different tasks. The difference is that when we are learning something new for the first time, we tend to process and recall the new material through our preferred brain hemisphere. If we receive data through our preferred side of the brain, it is more automatic, natural, and easier for us to improve our memory.

Storing Information: Step-by-Step or Simultaneously

When we learn something new, we also will find it easier if the material is presented in a way that matches the way we *store* and *remember* information. The left side of the brain stores and recalls it in a sequential, step- by-step order. The left side absorbs and recalls information in a linear order, bit by bit, one piece at a time. It has difficulty getting the big picture unless information is presented sequentially. The right side of the brain stores and recalls information in a simultaneous, global way; it sees the whole picture or main idea at once. It has difficulty receiving and recalling information in a step-by-step way unless it gets the big picture. Both sides of the brain are equally important, have their role to play in human life, and must work together.

Are there people who can store and recall the information both ways? Yes. These people have developed the use of both sides of the brain. They are equally comfortable with both left-brain linear thinking and remembering and right-brain global thinking and remembering. Those who do not use both sides of the brain, who favor one side, need to know their preference in order to find out how to improve memory quickly.

The characteristics of both sides of the brain will be described in the chapters on the eight superlinks. Keep in mind that few people use only one side exclusively. Thus, few people have *all* the characteristics described for either right-brain or left- brain learners. The higher you score for a left-brain preference, the closer you come to the description of the left-brain characteristics. The higher you score for a right-brain preference, the closer you will be to the description of characteristics of the right brain learner.

If you use both right- and left-brain functions equally, or you have a mixed preference in which you used the right side of the brain for certain tasks and the left side for others, then in the section on the eight superlinks you will need the chapters on both left-brain learners and right-brain learners because you have characteristics of both. You can highlight the aspects of each side of the brain that apply to you.

If you use both sides of the brain equally, also read Chapter 7 that describes the integrated use of both sides of your brain. If you were right-brain for certain tasks, and left-brain for others, refer to Chapter 8 for a description of the characteristics of having a mixed preference. This data is important because you are identifying how *you* need to remember. In the later chapters, you will be applying this information to remember anything quickly.

Although intuition has been traditionally considered as a function of the right side of the brain, research has not confirmed this. What is perceived to be intuition could actually be a function of reading nonverbal communication, synthesizing unrelated material and events into a whole, or using one's imagination, creating thinking, or inventive abilities.

Both right- brained and-left brain people may have intuition. Future studies may reveal that intuition may be beyond the scope of the right or left hemispheres of the brain.

Each year we discover new things about the brain. As new studies arise, current data is subject to change. We must continually revise our existing knowledge as these new findings arise.

CHAPTER 7:
INTEGRATED RIGHT AND LEFT-BRAIN
LEARNERS

People who have developed the ability to use both sides of their brain to remember are called integrated right- and left-brain learners. They use each side appropriately for the task. For tasks more easily accomplished by the right side of the brain, they use right-brain functions. Conversely, for tasks easily handled by the left side of the brain, they use the left side of the brain. Thus, this group of people learns easily in any kind of environment, a left- or right-brain one.

How to Develop an Integrated Brain Style through the Power of Brain Plasticity

If we develop both sides of the brain, we can make fuller use of our potential. We can continue to increase the capabilities of our brain to remember through the power of brain plasticity; it is never too late to work on our weaker side, although to improve memory of a subject more quickly we still want to learn through our preferred side of the brain. However, during those off-hours when we are not trying to remember something new, we can engage in activities that stimulate the other side of the brain. Thus, left-brain learners may want to spend some time daily in right-brain activities, and vice versa. You can read through the descriptions of the right-brain visual, auditory, tactile, and kinesthetic learners to find out what activities they do and spend some time in some of them, each day, to develop the right side of your brain to improve memory. To develop the left side of the brain, read descriptions of the left- brain visual, auditory, tactile, and kinesthetic learners and start doing left-brain activities daily.

For example, left-brain learners can develop the right side of the brain by using their left hand to draw or write (if they are not already left-handed), by playing games that involve finding missing numbers or shapes to complete a pattern, or by playing word games in which they make as many words as possible by mixing up a set of given letters. Other activities include brainstorming, inventing, or doing creative writing. Another way to develop the right side of the brain is through reading people's nonverbal expressions such as facial gestures, tones of voice, and body language, such as through turning off the sound on a DVD or television program to figure out the feelings behind the actors' and actresses' gestures. One can also take new routes to work or put away the clock and living without paying attention to time for a whole day.

Right-brain people can develop left-brain skills by using their right hand for drawing, writing, or doing activities (if they are not already right-handed). To develop the left brain's sequential, step-by-step abilities, one activity is to read a story or article and first make a right-brain mind map showing the main ideas in a large circle, with all the supporting details in smaller circles radiating as if spokes off the main ideas. Next, convert the mind map into a traditional left-brain outline format in a linear, sequential way. Other ways to develop the left side of the brain is to get a file cabinet and file your papers alphabetically or chronologically, or get a planning book or calendar, write in your appointments, and set as a goal to keep each one on time. Get a watch or beeper and program it to go off as a reminder to keep your appointments, or your to-do list, on time.

The following are characteristics of integrated left- and right-brain learners:

Understanding the World: Integrated left- and right-brain learners can think in terms of symbols and language as well as sensory experiences. When asked to see blue, they may see both the color and the letters that spell the word *blue*. They can remember sensory impressions as they would see a movie in their heads and can also use words and symbols to think about what they perceived. Their lives are enriched because they can think, recall, and process in both symbolic language such as words, symbols, and ideas, and in pictorial language and sensory input. Just as someone who is bilingual can communicate in two languages with a wider range of people, integrated learners can move easily from one environment to another and can understand people and subjects who communicate both in a right- and left-brain manner.

Remembering Material: Integrated left- and right-brain thinkers remember information both simultaneously in a step-by-step way. Thus, they can grasp the big picture in a simultaneous way, and go back and file its details in a sequential way. At times, they may work in a wholistic way, thinking about the big picture. At other times, they may organize and recall their ideas or papers in a step-by-step way, alphabetically, numerically, or in some order that makes sense to them. This ability gives them the added advantage of picking the memory storage system that matches the task.

This flexibility also enables them to remember from both

a right brain, global presentation as well as from a left-brain step-by-step linear presentation. When they present data, they do it in either a simultaneous or step-by-step way.

Sense of Time: Integrated left- and right-brain learners are aware of time. They can hide out in the right side of the brain and become oblivious of time, or they can be very scheduled when they shift over to attending to the functions of the left side of the brain. Thus, they can also pick and choose whether they will live according to a schedule or become lost in timelessness. With experience, they learn which situations require a sense of time and which do not.

Visual-Spatial Relationships: The right side of the brain gives integrated left- and right-brain learners the ability to deal with visual-spatial relationships with good perception of color, shape, and design. They are aware of and recall the relation of objects and people in space.

Creativity and Imagination: Integrated right- and-left-brain learners can deal with two types of creativity and imagination. They can work with existing forms and objects or ideas and put them together in new ways, or they can create something new. With full use of their brain, they have a wide range of options open to them.

Communication: Integrated left- and right-brain thinkers can listen through both sides of the brain. Thus, they are hearing the words and picking up nonverbal cues as well. This makes them more aware and conscious of what is happening around them than those who only receive information through one side of the brain. Thus, integrated left- and right-brain learners are attending to the meaning of the words as well as the hidden meaning expressed by a speaker's tones of voice, or facial and body gestures. This ability allows them to communicate both articulately and empathetically with expressive gestures or tones of voice.

Whole-to-Part and Part-to-Whole Thinking: Integrated left and right-brain learners can look at and recall information in both ways. They can start with the big picture and then go back and analyze the details, or they can go through the details in a linear way and then understand the sum total at the end. They can look at a book from front to back as well as back to front, or by skipping around, and be equally as happy. This fluidity of thought enables them to function in different types of learning environments with different instructors.

Synthesis vs. Analysis: Integrated left- and right- brain learners can move comfortably between analyzing and synthesizing. They can break down an idea or process into its component parts and put them back together in the same or in a new way. This makes them ideal inventors and creators. They are adept at finding new solutions to problems, creating new gadgets or inventions, finding new ways to create in the arts, or new ways to look at the world. They can look at their new synthesized creations and inventions in an analytical way so they can test it out and examine it for flaws and correct it. These people can see the total synthesized idea or product and analyze its parts to ensure that no aspect of a project or product has been left out.

The Challenges of Having an Integrated Left- and Right-Brain Style of Learning

With capabilities on both sides of the brain, the challenges of having an integrated left- and right-brain learning style means that one may feel there are two ways of thinking and remembering inside one's head, each competing for attention. These multi-ways of thinking and remembering make people so diverse and talented, with so many interests, that they can feel overwhelmed by their own capabilities and find it hard to prioritize. They have so much they want to do, so many people to meet and places to see, that they cannot do everything they want to do. They feel limited by the number of hours in a day and number of years in their lives. This creates its own kind of frustration, because with expanded capabilities there is so much they want to accomplish in so little time.

Benefits of Having an Integrated Left- and Right-Brain Brain Learning Style

One of the greatest plusses of having integrated use of both sides of the brain is in the area of discovery, invention, and creation. The right side of the brain can create new art forms and make new scientific discoveries and inventions, while the left side has the ability to communicate it to the world through language. There are some people who create something new but do not know how to get it across to others. Thus, it may just live and die with them. But having the ability to put one's creations or inventions into language to help others understand it, or to be able to write or speak about it in a sequential, logical way so that others can carry it further or do something with it, is an important quality to have. Thus, those with integrated use of both sides of the brain can make important contributions to humanity for others to understand and use.

CHAPTER 8:
RIGHT AND LEFT-BRAIN MIXED
PREFERENCES

Some people have a right-and-left-brain mixed preference, which means that they perform some functions with one side of the brain and other functions with the others side. When they use the side of the brain that matches the task, there is no problem. Mixed left- and right-brained preference learners just need to be aware of their strengths and know how to apply them to the task.

Sometimes people with a mixed preference use one side of the brain, but not necessarily in a way that matches the task. Some people use the right side of the brain for tasks that are better performed by the left side, and vice versa. Thus, these people may find their performance is not always at its best. At worst, it creates confusion and makes remembering a great struggle in certain situations. To provide strategies to alleviate the difficulties it may create, the rest of the chapter will focus on situations in which one is not using his or her brain in the best or most appropriate manner for the task, and what can be done about it.

Using the Right Side of the Brain for Left- Brain Tasks

Most academic subjects in schools that have been based on tasks such as reading, writing, spelling, grammar, public speaking, learning a foreign language, and doing certain math computation functions have been traditionally taught in a left-brain way, requiring understanding, and recalling abstract symbols such as numbers, letters, and words. People who use the right side of the brain when taught in this left-brain way find that it does not work and end up struggling. One reason these subjects are taught in a left-brain manner is that many people who became teachers and college instructors were people who succeeded in the educational system and could function well in this left-brain environment. Thus, when they taught the upcoming generation, they tended to use the same techniques—left- brain methods—that helped them learn and remember the material when they were students. However, all the subjects listed below can be taught in a right-brain manner so that right-brain people can be successful.

Right-brain techniques are presented later in this book, which gives right-brain memory, reading, comprehension, study skills, note taking, and test-taking skills and strategies for remembering anything quickly.

Reading Comprehension: People with right-brain preferences read, comprehend, and remember differently than those who read with the left side of their brain. Right-brain people learn to read more easily through recognizing repeated patterns, such as phonemic or phonics patterns, in which they read, for example, at, fat, cat, hat, and so forth, and can then remember the sound that any other word with at makes when they see it in other words. They also respond to sensory words that invoke strong images processed in the right side of the brain. Thus, when they read, they are going after the big picture, the main points, the strong visual images, actions, sounds, and feelings. There is nothing wrong with reading in this manner unless you have to attend to details, abstract ideas, or small words that can change the meaning of the text. It also causes difficulties when one has to perform an important test or task. Even if a right-brain person gets the main idea of what they read they may end up struggling with final examinations, high school or college entrance exams or placements tests (GED, ACT, SAT, GRE, etc.), certification tests, qualifying tests, or tests of reading abilities. They are placed at a disadvantage and low scores may mean anything from failure, to low-self- esteem, to not getting admitted into the school of their choice and sadly, to dropping out. If a right-brain learner's career depends on certification, it could also affect his or her future. There are two options available to right-brain people who have to perform on a left-brain reading activity or test. One is to develop their left-brain skills. The second is to convert the task into a right-brain one so as to perform well on it. Without this training, right-brain people may pass through a good portion of their lives needlessly struggling with reading, comprehension, or memory; feeling like failures; or missing many opportunities to advance themselves and their career.

Spelling: Spelling is another task that requires writing letters in order, a left-brain function. Again, those who are using the right side of the brain for spelling will often find themselves mixing up letters because the right brain does not work in sequential order. This means that they may be a good writer, but in school or job situations, people will see their poor spelling and may disregard their writing abilities. However, I have taught many right-brain people to spell using right-brain memory techniques.

Grammar: Poor grammar can reflect on one's writing abilities, speaking abilities, and educational background. A right-brain learner may be brilliant, but if he or she does not speak or write grammatically, others will not know the depth of his or her intelligence. Again, right-brain students again struggle and find themselves getting low test scores when it comes to tasks involving grammar even though they may have brilliant ideas, because grammar requires attention to details and sequential order. Right-brain people can use right-brain techniques, however, to master grammar.

Writing: Right-brain learners may have creative ideas, but much of writing in schools and on the job is evaluated according to left-brain rules and criteria. Thus, organization and logical structure, writing ideas in sequence, correct sentence structure, and correct use of the mechanics of writing are left-brain functions. Right-brain people can become excellent writers by using right-brain techniques to master this left-brain skill.

Foreign Language: Foreign language studies require success in reading, writing, spelling, speaking, and grammar. It also requires the storage of two languages in the brain. People who use the right side of the brain to learn a foreign language may find themselves struggling with certain left-brain tasks. Thus, for example, if one wants to learn how to remember Spanish quickly, or learn how to recall French or German, or any other language, quickly, knowing how to use right-brain techniques can help with mastering left-brain skills.

Math: Certain math tasks pose another problem for people who use the right side of the brain. Many math problems can be done with right-brain techniques. Right-brain learners can grasp the whole picture, identifying patterns, and seeing interconnections. But when the task is presented in a text that requires reading instructions or word problems that must be solved through a step-by-step method, right-brain learners tend to struggle. Even when they can get the correct answer for a problem, they often do not get credit because they did not write how they got the results in a left-brain detailed and sequential way. Often, they are penalized for being unable to explain, in words, how they arrived at an answer.

Sometimes people with a strong right-brain preference may transpose numbers. They know what number they are writing, but when they write, two numbers often come out transposed or totally backward. This happens because the right side of the brain sees the whole number simultaneously, while it is the left side of the brain that puts the digits in order. When a right-brain person does not take the time to double-check a number, it may come out mixed up. Thus, tasks involving accuracy of computation may suffer. Through using right-brain techniques a right-brain learner can master those tasks in math that require left-brain processes.

Jobs: Many jobs require attention to order and detail such as computer programming, accounting, being a bank teller or a cashier, engineering, or proofreading, to name a few. People who have a mixed preference should be aware that they might need to use the left side of the brain to perform left-brain tasks or use right-brain adaptations for the left-brain task.

Right brain adaptations are given later in this book, which focuses on learning by using your best superlink memory and learning style and brain style to succeed.

Using the Left Side of the Brain for Right-Brain Tasks

When someone with a mixed left- and right-brain preference has been in the habit of using the left side of the brain to perform right-brain tasks, they may struggle just as those who use the right side of the brain do when performing left-brain tasks. Here are some situations in which using the left brain may impede performance of a right-brain task.

In offices or planning sessions, brainstorming is often a desirable way to generate ideas and solutions for problems. The session requires letting one's mind stay open to various possibilities. It is a time in which suggestions on the floor can trigger other associations and ideas. Someone with a mixed left- and right-brain preference may end up engaging the left side of the brain and hindering the brainstorming session. Instead of staying open to all possible suggestions, the left-brainer will begin judging and analyzing each suggestion in a microscopic way, arguing why it would or would not work. The brainstorming session is not the time for judging and evaluating the details of each idea.

Interrupting a right-brain brainstorming session—a right-brain task—can bog down the process and stop the free-flow of ideas needed to find solutions. The left brain needs to reserve its analytical abilities for a later time, after the brainstorming is over, when the specific suggestions are looked at for their practicality.

In tasks such as art, music, new product design, movie production, science and technology, or advertising, which involve creating or inventing something new, left-brain learners may have a hard time. They are stuck with the ideas and concepts they already know and cannot make a leap into the new and unknown. They would rather produce a step-by-step instruction manual of a process they know than explore unknown territory. They would rather be told what to do or follow directions than have the freedom to create anything they want. They need to learn to develop the right side of the brain's simultaneous thinking to help them with new ideas, make new connections, and imagine new possibilities. They must adapt the right-brain task to the left side of the brain and use their own step-by-step approach to come up with new ideas, or develop the right side of their brain.

Many tasks require the right side of the brain.

People with mixed preferences may be using the left side for tasks that would be better serviced by the right side of the brain. They, too, need to know which side is appropriate for which task so they can use that side appropriately. Left-brain adaptations are given later in this book, which focuses on techniques for remembering by using your best superlink memory and learning style and brain style to improve memory to master any subject.

Mistaken Identity: Is it a Learning Disability or Just Not Matching the Side of the Brain to a Task?

Many people grow up thinking they have a memory or learning problem or a learning disability when in fact they are just using the wrong techniques to learn. Even today there are thousands of students who are classified as learning disabled or having problems with memory when, in fact, a task is not presented in a way that is compatible with their brain hemispheric preference, or they have not been taught how to use the side of the brain that matches the task. A learning disability is a dysfunction of the central nervous system, which means there is impairment in the circuitry between the senses, the nervous system, and the brain. This impairment can be thought of as a short circuit in the nervous system that scrambles a message as it travels from the senses to the brain and back to the senses. This situation does not apply to someone with a mixed preference who has no central nervous system dysfunction, but who has simply not been taught how to use the right side of the brain for right-brain tasks or the left side of the brain for left-brain tasks. Someone with a mixed preference may appear to make the same mistake as someone with a learning disability, but there is a world of difference. The learning-disabled person has damage to the central nervous system which to date is not repairable (but science may find a way to repair it in the future). Thus, no matter how many times they do the same task they will not get it. They have to learn how to accomplish the task using different sensory modalities or techniques. Someone with a mixed left- and right-brain preference can learn how to use the other side of the brain or can convert the task to match the side of the brain for which they show a preference. It is not a question of damage, but one of usage. They have been using one side of the brain since childhood causing it to develop more neural connections, resulting in making that side more efficient and rapid. The other side of the brain also can be developed, or the task can be restructured to match the preferred side.

Many people with a mixed left- and right-brain preference use each side of the brain inappropriately for certain tasks and thus may have grown up thinking there was something wrong with them or their memories. This may affect their self-esteem and their motivation to succeed, and they may have actually dropped out of school or not continued on to higher education thinking there was something wrong to them. Only as an adult do many people with mixed preference discover that they are not dumb or stupid, or lack a good memory, but that the system they used failed them. They discover that when the instruction matches their memory and learning style and brain style they are excellent learners. It is only the approach used during their school career that was wrong, and with a new approach they can finally feel success. Later in this book you will learn how to convert the language of each side of the brain into the other as a way to make memory skills easier and faster.

PART 4:
YOUR SUPERLINK TO HOW TO IMPROVE YOUR MEMORY TO LEARN ANY SUBJECT QUICKLY

CHAPTER 9:

CREATE YOUR PERSONAL SUPERLINK MEMORY LEARNING STYLE AND BRAIN STYLE PROFILE

As you read about the eight Superlinks in the following chapters, you will learn about your own memory superlink and form a profile of how you remember. You should jot down information as you read about your superlink or combination of memory and learning links in the next eight chapters. As you advance further in the book, you will use this data, applying this knowledge to improve memory of any subject quickly.

You may find that the chapter on your own superlink describes you completely. If you are a combination of two or more memory and learning styles, you may also discover that there are portions of several chapters that accurately describe you. This means that your personal profile will contain memory and learning strategies suited for you from a combination of your superlinks memory and learning and brain styles. For example, you may have found that you are a combination of two superlinks: tactile left brain and visual left brain. Thus, your personal profile will contain portions of those two chapters.

Since we use each of our senses and both sides of our brain to varying degrees, many combinations of superlinks are possible. Do not feel you have to fit precisely into one category. You may remember through a combination of several Superlinks memory and learning styles. Some people may be fortunate enough to have developed their whole brain and find that all eight memory and learning links fit them!

The descriptions of each superlink given in the next eight chapters are not meant to restrict options for people or form stereotypes. Anyone with any memory and learning and brain style can function well at any task and in any job either by adapting to the situation, by approaching the job in a different way, or bringing his or her own unique perspective to it.

If you find that you use a combination of superlinks, pick out the portions from each superlink chapter that apply to you and take notes on that portion. The essential point is that you know what *your* particular combination means for *your* memory, and know how *you* can use it to improve memory and apply it to any subject such as reading comprehension, study skills, note taking, and test taking skills. In this way, you will have in hand your own personal profile to refer to as you move through the rest of this book.

Directions: If you have taken the Superlinks Linksman Learning Style and Brain Hemispheric Preference assessment tests, and know your superlink style, you can go right to your chapter or chapters related to you. Alternatively, if you did not take the superlinks assessment, you can still read all the chapters on each superlink in this book and as you find one or more that fit you, highlight or take notes on the portions of each that describe how you need to remember. This will give you an actionable plan to improve your memory in any subject.

CHAPTER 10:
WHAT IS A VISUAL LEFT-BRAIN LEARNER AND HOW TO IMPROVE YOUR MEMORY QUICKLY?

What is a Visual Left-Brain Learner?

Visual left-brain learners take in information through their eyes and comprehend and remember by converting it into symbols or language, such as letters, numbers, words, or ideas. Although they are sensitive to their visual environment, they pay particular attention to printed matter—letters, words, or numbers. They mentally label this sensory information with names and words. They think, comprehend, and remember in a step- by-step way, attending to one detail at a time, and file data in a systematic way, whether alphabetically, numerically, or chronologically.

Since they like to stay organized, they are often engaged in organizing materials involving words and numbers. They may spend time filing their papers, organizing phone numbers and addresses, keeping their finances up to date, paying bills, doing budgets, scheduling appointments in their offices or homes, keeping up with correspondence, programming their computers, doing spreadsheets, or making sure birthday and anniversary cards are mailed out on time. They may find organized and efficient ways for setting up accounting, payroll, record-keeping, or book-keeping systems.

To keep their life in order, they may make charts and graphs. They are good at keeping company records, archiving, setting appointments, making chronologies and timelines, keeping timetables and scheduling, and other such tasks. They do not miss a detail and seldom miss an appointment, as long as it is written so they can see it.

When they are traveling, they plan everything they are going to see in detail in advance. They collect travel brochures, schedules, and information and make reservations far in advance. They like to stick to their planned schedules and feel uncomfortable when anything interferes with anything that they have already visualized and planned in their minds.

How Visual Left-Brain Learners Can Improve Memory to Accelerate Learning

Visual left-brain people can improve memory to accelerate their learning by reading and seeing visual materials in the form of language: letters, words, and numbers. They also need eye contact with a speaker.

They recall any subject more quickly through reading books and study guides if the information is organized and clearly written in step-by-step order. To learn a language, they need to see a vocabulary word, its definition, and visual clues for its pronunciation. To learn math, they need to read step-by-step instructions showing them how to do a problem. They tend to be accurate with mathematical calculations. Self-study programs that require reading are excellent for them.

Visual left-brain learners learn through the written word, whether through physically printed versions, eBooks, or digital downloads? They learn well through seeing books, magazines, journals, newspapers, technical manuals, guidebooks, instruction books, or power point presentations or viewing other media that has printed words presented through the computer, DVDs with textual captions, CDs, or audio downloads with accompanying printed text manuals. Reading tables, graphs, charts, and posters are helpful. Written communication is a way to get a message across to them. They are quicker at responding to text messages, social media posts or blogs, E-mail, faxes, written directions, memos, or letters than to phone calls or verbal communications. Computer programs and electronic communication networks that require reading texts with step-by-step detailed instructions are ideal for visual left- brain learners.

Visual left-brain people can study with music, noise, or talking in the background because they are so focused visually that they can tune out those distractions.

Due to their keen sensitivity to visual stimuli, they are bothered by visual clutter or disorganization in print material. They recall what they have seen and can spot whether print looks right to them. It is as if they have an automatic spell checker in their brain. They make excellent proofreaders and copyeditors. They can also spot errors in numerical information such as financial reports, budgets, paychecks, tax returns, restaurant checks, or spreadsheets. These are the people who will take a red pen to circle other people's errors. (It might have been a visual left-brain person who invented proofreader's markings!)

They can learn and remember the rules of writing, grammar, punctuation, and spelling if the material is presented in order with rules and formulas printed out. They can visually recall examples they see in a textbook. They need everything in their visual environment to look right, especially printed material.

How-to, step-by-step books and guides written in a clear, sequential manner improve their comprehension and memory to accelerate the visual left-brain person's learning. They can learn how to fix a motor, cook a meal, build an addition to a home, or run a business by reading about it rather than merely observing it.

When working on projects or solving problems, visual left-brain learners should outline or sequentially list the steps they need to do to reach the solution so they can *see* their plan on paper, and make sure they have everything they need to carry out each part of the task.

Visual left-brain people can make excellent administrators and managers because they are extremely organized and can see a task through to completion.

Visual left-brain learners like to learn according to a schedule and deadlines. Keeping an organizer, calendar, or Day-Timer is ideal for them so they can see their schedule.

To improve reading, visual left brain learners must visualize the words and details they read. Although reading words can be taught through any Superlinks style, traditionally it has been taught as a visual, sequential activity based on interpreting symbols, making reading easy for visual left-brain people because they process and organize information that way. As they read, they visually record every word in their brain in order and can recall the material when questioned. Thus, they tend to do well on tests based on memorization of reading material. Visual left-brain learners are good test takers if they have study guides, notes, textbooks, or test prep books from which to study. For example, as students they need ACT, SAT, or High School Placement Test prep books and college or career prep study guides with text to do practice reading tests so they can *see* what the tests will look like. Some visual left- brain learners are like walking encyclopedias. Ask them to find a fact and they will not only recall what book they read it in, but where in the book they saw it and what visual material surrounded what they read. They are good at skimming to find needed data.

They often read as if they were a computer spelling or fact checker. They will immediately notice that something looks wrong or does not match the original data. This makes them careful readers of details, either words or numbers.

Because visual left-brain learners focus well on details, their learning is slowed down when they have to condense or summarize the gist of what they read to get the main idea. Thus, they do better on recall of facts they read than on getting the big picture or making inferences, since these are unstated and they have not *seen* them written in the text.

In the work force, dealing with print material, either in words or in numbers, is ideal for them. In the world of words, they can be found in: administration, management, office work such as preparing reports, filing, assistant work, scheduling, appointment setting, areas dealing with time-management and efficiency, publishing, writing, editing, proofreading, teaching, research in any field, library work, writing copy for advertising, marketing or sales, writing technical and instructional manuals, reviews, and literary criticism, and so on. In the world of numbers, they can be found in accounting, business, finance, stock brokerages, tax specialization, banking, budgeting, economics, financial planning, insurance, payroll, teaching mathematics, statistics, evaluation and measurement, market research, and computer programming.

In any career, such as medicine, law, engineering, IT, social services, education, or running a business, there are numerous tasks involving sequential thinking, which left-brain visual people find matches how they work best.

Adapting Instruction to a Visual Left-Brain Learning Style to Improve Memory

Because visual-left brain learners focus well on details, they should ask for instruction in the form of outlines, study guides, or notes in sequential order on a white board, power point presentation, online lesson, or paper. In this way, they can see what is important, read along, or organize the information in their mind. They can improve their study skills by taking notes on what they read. If the instructor in lecturing they can take dictation in a sequential organized way, such as by outlining or making a graphic organizer, so later they can *see* their notes or visualize it in their mind. They may need to find their own sequentially written books and materials that corresponds with the subject to read in order to learn it quickly on their own.

CHAPTER 11:
WHAT IS A VISUAL RIGHT-BRAIN LEARNER AND HOW TO IMPROVE YOUR MEMORY QUICKLY?

What Is a Visual Right Brain Learner?

To learn and remember quickly, visual right-brain learners take in information through their eyes and comprehend and remember best in the form of images, pictures, graphics, colors, shapes, faces, designs, sizes, and spatial relations. They process and think about visual stimuli in a simultaneous or global way, seeing the whole picture at once. Only after they grasp the big picture can they focus on its details.

Visual right-brain learners are attuned to the way things look and are bothered by visual clutter. They notice when the colors in a room do not match or if an object is out of place. They make good interior decorators, and with their keen sense of visual balance and design they have a good eye for what accessories go together in a room. They can rearrange a room until it looks visually pleasing. This same sensitivity makes them notice how people look and dress. They like clothes that look good and use their great eye for color and design to select matching clothes and accessories. They enjoy having their own clothes, skin, hair, or face look good as well as making others look good. Some may tell others when their hair is out of place, their tie does not match the suit, or a button is open. They are so keenly aware of how things look they can become distracted unless the disturbing visual appearance is fixed.

They like to produce work that looks visually appealing in design and color. These are the people to whom others come for attractive presentation packets, color graphics, attractively bound reports, and visual aids. Visual right-brain learners are the ones who beautify the world. They will hang paintings in a room, keep attractive posters or art around the office, and bring in the flower arrangements. People call on them to decorate the office for the staff party.

They may like going to art galleries, photo exhibits, fashion shows, or auto shows, or going sightseeing. They may get pleasure from looking at beautiful homes, gardens, cars, boats, horse, or animal shows—anything that can be seen. They may enjoy the visuals of the theater, a circus, a museum, a zoo, a park, gardens, or amusement or theme parks with fascinating sights to see.

While they do not keep their things in an organized, linear way like their left-brain counterparts do, they want their visual surroundings to be appealing and will find a way to keep their things in an attractive way. Although they may not be from the filers, they will have attractive organizers such as colorful boxes, stylish containers, decorative pencil holders, and storage units for their belongings, even if within these containers, its contents are not organized sequentially.

Visual right-brain learners go with the flow and end up being in the flow, often becoming so absorbed in their visual projects that they lose track of time. Thus, they can start and finish work on their own time according to the demands of the project rather than the clock.

How Visual Right-Brain Learners Can Improve Memory Quickly

The best way for visual right-brain learners to improve memory to learn anything quickly is by using visual aids with graphic and pictorial content that allows them to see the big picture. They learn from or remember text or numbers better if they are presented using color, shape, design, special calligraphy, or an artistic font.

Many visual-right learners do not respond to verbal instructions and will find it difficult until given visual directions on paper with pictorial images, diagrams, or charts. Pure lecture does not work because they have to work hard at concentrating on auditory stimuli. When they can see a speaker, graphics, and visual aids, their best learning modality is open. To understand and recall verbal lectures or oral communication, visual right-brain learners need to receive these coupled with visual stimuli. They learn and remember better by having eye contact with a speaker rather than listening to an audiotaped lecture, but the speaker must also give them something to look at in pictorial form.

If they do not have anything to look at and find themselves in an auditory teaching situation, visual right- brain learners can adapt by listening to the descriptive words in the lecture so they can paint a mental picture for themselves. They will have a hard time understanding what others are saying unless they are provided with descriptions of color, size, or shape to visualize in their mind.

Visual right-brain learners need to see visual aids such as graphics and pictures found in printed or digital books or eBooks, magazines, newspapers, hand-outs, power points, online lessons, notes on a flip chart, white board, or chalkboard. It helps for them to see colorful posters, art work, charts, maps, diagrams, graphs, visual displays, or overheads. They require illustrations, pictures, drawings, paintings, photographs, slide shows, DVDs, television, movies, live examples, real-life objects, demonstrations, and enactments with visual and scenic imagery, so they can see what you are talking about to help them understand and learn. They like computer programs or apps with good graphics and visual images that operate using icons and pictorial directions, rather than detailed, sequential directions.

When describing events or experiences from the past, visual right-brain learners will recall images they saw in real life, movies, photographs, and videos, the surroundings, and what people looked like. They are great at spotting famous personalities and people they know in different contexts by matching visual features.

Visual right-brain learners need to see objects or pictures of what you want them to do. Draw a garbage can or a broom if you want your teens to take out the trash or sweep their room. Hang posters and charts with pictorial diagrams of the steps to follow as visual reminders of your instructions. When explaining a medical procedure, doctors and dentists should give visual right-brain patients a simple pictorial chart or diagram with few words in which everything can be seen on one page. Just writing the words will not get it across to them unless there is a picture with it.

It is easier for them to do math problems when there is a photograph or pictorial image to accompany the problem as an example. If you are multiplying 24 x 3, they want to see a picture of twenty-four people each holding three slices of pizza.

Using intuition, experimentation, and discovery, they can uncover new ways to do things and find solutions for problems. They make associations easily and one image will bring others to mind. This makes them good at learning through brainstorming or making connections. Since they think things through in a simultaneous way, before starting a project, they first need to know the end product, goal, or bottom line. Once they see the big picture, the connections between every part makes sense to them. After they see the big picture they are impatient with step-by-step directions and want to jump in and figure it for themselves as they do it.

Visual right-brain people can improve their reading by converting every word of text into images so they can see what they are reading in their head. This dramatically improves their reading comprehension. It is hard for the visual right-brain learner to grasp words that do not invoke images, such as articles like *a* and *the*, verb tenses, or prepositions. Many tend to focus on words that can be pictured and skip over these small abstract words that cannot be pictured, like *the*, *that*, or *and*, or substituting *the* for *a*, or vice versa. Thus, on a test, they often score higher on questions that contain visual imagery and lower on those that cannot be visualized. If they need to pass an examination or master abstract material, they need to develop the right-brain technique for visualizing everything, even abstract words.

They prefer books that use descriptive words that help them paint a picture in their mind as well as books with illustrations, graphics, photographs, and other visual aids. They do not like detailed, sequential books, but those that get to the point with images, people, and happenings they can see. To accelerate learning, they need to select books that give a global overview and are supplemented by graphics and pictorial images to increase understanding.

In the work force, you may find visual right-brain people engaged in the fine arts or graphic design. With their expert eye, they may be artists, illustrators, painters, sculptors, jewelry makers, clothing designers, fashion illustrators, interior decorators, beauticians, aestheticians, cosmetologists, or hair-dressers. They may be involved with graphic arts, computer graphics, and commercial illustration, advertising, or designing posters, brochures, sales pieces, or billboards. In the publishing world, they may be the art directors, children's book illustrators, the layout and graphic designers, and those that make beautiful books. They make good photographers and you will find their work beautifying magazines, books, brochures, booklets, and other print or digital media.

Other activities in which they may find enjoyment are floral arranging, landscaping, or architecture. They want their visual surroundings to be beautiful. They may be the ones to design stationery, greeting cards, or new forms of calligraphy or typography fonts.

As engineers they want to design buildings, structures, or transportation vehicles that look good. They make good car designers, coming up with new sleek, beautiful models.

If involved in others fields, such as medicine, law, education, the sciences, social service, businesses, sales, finance, marketing, sports, the performing arts, music, and so on, they will learn best through visual right-brain strategies and bring a sense of color, design, artistic sensibility, and beauty to whatever endeavor in which they engage.

Adapting Instruction to a Visual Right-Brain Memory and Learning and Brain Style

Visual right-brain learners need to ask instructors to provide visual images showing the global overview.

They need to see the big picture using pictorial images, mind maps, real-life objects or demonstrations, or find their own visual materials. Since auditory presentations are difficult for visual right-brain learners, they need to see a) a written copy of a lecture; or b) do their own note taking so they can read at their own pace, converting each word into: a mental image; a colorful illustration; a mind map of the main topic, its details, and their interconnections; or words and numbers written in colorful, decorative calligraphy or design so they can *see* the material.

CHAPTER 12:
WHAT IS AN AUDITORY LEFT-BRAIN LEARNER AND HOW TO IMPROVE YOUR MEMORY QUICKLY?

What Is an Auditory Left-Brain Learner?

An auditory left-brain learner learns and remembers best and more quickly by hearing the new material presented in the form of language, either words or numbers, in a detailed, step-by-step way. They also think by speaking their thoughts aloud and conversing aloud with others. They work well with accurate data, facts, figures, and statistics and can make excellent researchers, often backing up their lectures and presentations, with information that supports their topic and gets their ideas across.

Auditory left-brain learners are sensitive to the quality of other people's speech, noticing mistakes in dialogue, such as grammatical and syntactical errors, poor usage of words, repetitive phrases, and poor delivery. They become uncomfortable when speakers drone on or use repetitive language, inappropriate pauses, or too many ums. Being conscious of speech, they are careful to be good speakers themselves and make great orators. They plan out and rehearse what they are going to say, making sure their sentences are grammatically correct and their language is precise and clear, with appropriate word choices. Many are conscious of timing and phrasing, pausing at the right place for added effect and modulating their voices in a way to keep their audiences engaged. They also make good editors, not for finding visual errors in spelling, but for being conscious of how the text should sound when read aloud. They enjoy collecting words and relish putting them together in interesting ways. They like fancy words, such as *cogitate* for *think*, and words that sound good and provide the closest shade of meaning.

They are great conversationalists and enjoy talking to a wide range of people. Their great auditory recall manifests itself in their speech when they quote other people like an automatic verbal playback system, replaying conversations almost word-for-word. They can be the life of the party with their storehouse of humorous anecdotes, interesting tidbits from current events and history, the wit and wisdom they heard from others, and their excellent verbal presentation skills. They can relate famous quotations, jokes, riddles, tales, poetry, and lines from the classics, movies, or lectures almost verbatim.

Auditory left-brain learners need constant auditory stimulus. Unless studying, they cannot handle absolute silence. If it is too quiet, they feel uncomfortable and will provide the auditory sounds themselves so they have something to listen to by humming, singing, whistling, talking to themselves aloud, turning on a radio talk show, television, Internet webinar, Teleseminar, or audiotape lecture, or calling someone on the phone. In an office or classroom, when it is too quiet, auditory people will start talking, wanting to discuss everything. They will either ask the speaker many questions or talk to people nearby. If no one will respond to them they may start talking to themselves aloud. The only time they need silence is when they are studying or reading, because music, noise, or the talking of others distracts them from hearing their own thoughts.

Even though they do not maintain steady eye contact with a speaker because when listening people's eyes tend to move left and right in the direction of their ears, they are good listeners and will ask a speaker many questions. Although their discussions can become lengthy because they speak with much sequential, analytical detail, their questions make others feel understood and appreciated.

Because auditory left-brain learners process their thoughts by speaking aloud, some have a tendency to repeat aloud what people around them say, either in their own way or a better way. To others who do not understand them, this may be annoying, but auditory left- brain people are not doing this to be rude or to one-up or put down others; they only repeat what others say because it helps them think about it more clearly. They also seem to make a running commentary on everything that is happening around them, which may sound to others as if they are criticizing or analyzing everything.

While others may keep their thoughts to themselves, auditory left-brain learners tend to speak their thoughts aloud. They are not trying to be critical—it is as if a microphone were placed inside their head and others can hear their thoughts. Auditory left-brain learners may need to understand this tendency, lest they turn other people off unintentionally.

They work sequentially and keep their files and papers orderly. Some enjoy the sequential aspect of working with mathematics by doing number and logic puzzles and solving math problems in everyday life.

Some understand the highly mathematical and sequential processes involved in economics, stocks, taxes, and finances and enjoy reading financial papers and business journals, keeping up with the stock market and the business world. They like to keep their financial records, both personal and business, straight, and like to be organized at tax time to do their returns.

Left-brain auditory people who are musically inclined enjoy listening to music and going to concerts, theater, or musicals. Reading music is easier for them because it involves converting musical sounds into symbols and vice versa. When they listen to music they are conscious of the technical aspects and analyze it according to their high standards, judging its technical execution such as the arrangement or a singer's voice quality, which makes them excellent music critics.

How an Auditory Left-Brain Learner Can Improve Memory Quickly

Auditory left-brain learners can remember and learn quickly and best by listening and talking when ideas are presented sequentially. In the classroom or in seminars, they learn best through lectures, oral presentations, and discussion. They recall details of conversations, lists, words to a song, or anything else if it is told to them in a step-by-step way. Whether learning how to learn a language, fix a car, write a computer software program, or play a sport, they learn better by listening to directions than by watching someone else perform the task. To improve study skills and test taking skills to memorize material for a test, they need to hear the material, talk about it, reread it aloud, or record themselves reading aloud and then play it back several times.

They grasp the meaning of verbal communication quickly without having to convert it into pictures. They can closely follow a college lecture, a verbal training session on the job, or auditory directions, while others of different learning styles may be asking, "What did the speaker say? I don't get it." Auditory left-brain people usually find others clustering around them asking them to explain announcements given over a PA system or to repeat the new policies that the boss explained at a meeting.

This group can be found attending lectures and seminars, or taking the audiotaped or guided tours through museums. Some are so absorbed in listening to a lecture during a sightseeing trip that they forget to look at the actual sights!

Auditory presentations such as audio books, webinars, teleseminars, movies, or DVDs played through digital or electronic devices or computers, or though radio or television are good learning tools for auditory- left brain learners. They may relax by listening to news or talk shows on the radio while driving, or listening to the evening news or a documentary on television or over the Internet after work. They also enjoy reading books, news magazines, newspapers, Internet articles, blogs, postings, and professional journals because when they read they hear the words in their head. Computer or digital programs with voice, verbal presentations, or text they can read aloud themselves, presented in a step-by- step way, are the best learning tools for them.

Auditory left-brain learners can remember better and learn well from technical manuals and instructional guides if they read them aloud. They are also good at writing them. These are the people who know how to write computer software programs or can follow the directions to set-up newly-purchased electronic or computer equipment. If you do not already have an auditory left-brain friend, you may want to search for one, because these are the people who understand the way things work in this technological age, based on the language of words, numbers, and computer terminology carried out in a logical, step-by-step way.

Many enjoy history, current events, and biographies because these are sequential, chronological, and verbal genres.

They are sensitive to auditory distractions. When they are listening to a speaker, they become annoyed if anything distracts them. A passing car, a humming heater, or someone crunching chips will drive them out of their minds. Since they cannot tune out auditory distractions as visual people can, they carefully orchestrate their listening environment to hear only the speaker or only their own thoughts. They have a hard time concentrating or studying with background music and need quiet to read and study. Headphones or earplugs may help them concentrate when there is too much auditory distraction.

Many auditories enjoy debate. They work well in teams and cooperative groups that involve discussion and use this continual feedback to restructure and regroup their own thoughts.

To improve memory of what they read and comprehend better, auditory left-brain learners need to read aloud, read softly to themselves, or hear the words in their mind. Some of them, though, if asked to read silently will automatically subvocalize by moving their lips, whisper-read, or read softly anyway. They need to stop frequently and ask themselves questions about what they read, either aloud or by hearing the answers in their head. They also need to hear what they read in a step-by- step way to grasp the material. If they read material that jumps from one idea to another without any order, they need to restructure it in their minds by asking questions in order to convert it into a step-by-step process and form an outline or study guide. They do not enjoy books that ramble on going nowhere, but those that are sequentially organized and move to a logical conclusion or resolution.

In the work force, they can be found in jobs requiring listening and talking in a step-by-step way. They may be public speakers, sales and marketing people, medical doctors, nurse practitioners, lawyers, politicians, administrators, scientists, presenters, lecturers, college professors, teachers, disc jockeys, musicians, singers, songwriters, editors, writers, poets, actors and actresses, announcers, emcees, broadcasters such as television news anchors, sportscasters, or announcers for commercials or audiobook recordings.

Some who are mathematically included may become mathematicians, accountants, bookkeepers, bankers, financial planners, tax specialists, economists, and stockbrokers.

No matter what their careers, auditory left-brain people are the ones asked to do tasks that involve speaking, listening, or giving oral presentations and training to the staff, clients, or trainees, because oral presentations of words and numbers are their medium for communication with the world.

Adapting Learning to an Auditory Left-Brain Style to Improve Memory

Auditory left-brain learners should ask an instructor to present material in an auditory, sequential way through lectures and discussion to help them remember better. Auditory left-brain people should use audio books or, if not available, use printed or digital books or do their own note taking in a linear manner to read aloud or into a tape recorder to hear it played back. Studying with a partner or discussion group helps them *hear* the material.

CHAPTER 13:
WHAT IS AN AUDITORY RIGHT-BRAIN LEARNER AND HOW TO IMPROVE YOUR MEMORY QUICKLY?

What Is an Auditory Right-Brain Learner?

Auditory right-brain learners remember and learn best through hearing and are attuned to sounds, music, rhythms, and nonverbal tones of voice, and strong sensory words that give an overview or the big picture. This group is sensitive to sounds that others do not notice, such as fans humming, cars passing, or equipment noise. Musical harmony is important to them because they are particularly bothered by any dissonant sounds. They are attracted to beautiful sounds, sweet melodies, and pleasing voices and are repelled by annoying and grating sounds such as sirens, construction drills, or irritating voices.

They enjoy traveling to get away from the dissonant sounds of a city to spend time relaxing amidst the sounds of nature in the mountains, a forest, or by the ocean. To keep the sounds at home or in their office pleasant, many have a good selection of music for background. Some enjoy environmental sound recordings such as the soothing sounds of the ocean, gentle rain, chirping birds in the forest, or running brooks.

Auditory right-brain learners have a good ear for music. They enjoy going to concerts, musicals, jazz brunches, or music clubs, or religious and social ceremonies with musical services or presentations. They can hear a tune, remember it

113

exactly, and either sing it or use an instrument to play it perfectly by ear. Many auditory right-brain people in the music field may not have had any formal music training and cannot read music; they just make music and it sounds great.

They spend time practicing and creating their own songs and instrumentals. They may create by hearing a new song, tune, or whole symphony in their heads coming to them intuitively, and then can reproduce it with instruments or by singing. It is as if they are tapped into an internal audio player that creates new melodies and songs.

Auditory right-brainers get creative ideas for sound effects, often coming up with new types of sounds, new genres of music, new instruments, or new combinations of instruments and sounds, such as combining music and the sounds of nature.

Right-brain auditory learners feel uncomfortable with absolute silence unless listening to the silence— between words, in the pauses of songs, or in nature. But even in the silence, nature speaks to them. When not particularly listening to silence, they feel uncomfortable when there is no auditory stimulus. Thus, they will create it by turning on music, or making the auditory stimuli themselves, such as singing, humming, whistling, tapping a beat, making their mouth sound like instruments or sound effects, mimicking voices or people's accents, or doing impersonations or cartoon character's voices.

Although they do not maintain direct eye contact with a speaker, because their eyes move from side to side in the direction of their eyes, they are acutely aware of nonverbal communication and tones of voices. They can pick up on someone's negativity, hidden anger, resentment, and sarcasm.

Conversely, they can also pick up someone's sincerity and loving, caring, and kind attitude from their tone of voice and will immediately respond to that person. Others may think they are mind readers because they can grasp people's true meaning from subtle nuances of tone in face-to-face and telephone conversations, no matter what words are used to hide the speaker's feelings. Auditory right-brain people appear to be deep, not saying much, but understanding all.

They enjoy being with people who do not stress their verbal auditory system. Some like to talk a lot to friends about their interests and hobbies, getting to the main point quickly and changing topics frequently, while others like to be with people with whom they can relax, not have to talk much, and can communicate with few words or with strong sensory language.

How an Auditory Right-Brain Learner Can Improve Memory to Learn Anything Quickly

Auditory right brain learners can improve memory to learn anything quickly by listening to sound, music, and strong sensory language that gives an overview or big picture. They recall better and learn from the sounds of words more than from printed text.

When they are memorizing material for a test or speech, it is better for them to hear someone else read the material and pick it up from the other's intonation and voice quality, or to write down the information themselves and read it aloud, talk about it, or tape-record it so they can play it back slowly several times. They can remember and repeat words verbatim better if they are combined with music, rhymes, rhythm, catchy songs and tunes, jingles in commercials and advertisements, poetry, raps, beats, environmental sounds, or by mimicking distinctive voice qualities or accents. They recall a story conveyed in a musical, or the words to a song on DVD or music videos. As children, they may have learned the alphabet by singing the alphabet song or learned number facts by listening to children's songs. Their best learning pathway is open when words and numbers are tied to music.

This group, which is not attuned to symbolic, abstract language such as letters, words, and numbers in a step-by-step presentation, does not learn well from lectures unless a person gets to the point using sensory words. They need to hear the bottom line and whole concept of how things are interrelated without going into details. When other people's conversation becomes too abstract, detailed, and sequential, some auditory right- brain learners may either cut them off and say, I get it, because they have grasped the whole idea or they tune out, drift off, hear a song in their head, hum it softly, tap the beat, or even sing it while the other person is still speaking. They will refocus on the lecture only when the speaker gets to the main point.

Live music, music recordings, Internet or multi- media presentations with music, movies, DVDs, television, computer programs, video games, and apps with good music and sound effects are the best learning materials for them. Sound makes these more enjoyable for them. Imaginative, interactive, and nonsequential computer programs and apps that can use sound effects, voice, and music are also good.

They understand better when words are tied to movies, DVDs, and real-life demonstrations because of the right brain's excellent visual-spatial memory. They can comprehend and remember better by mentally converting words into a movie in their heads, with imagined music, sound effects, and dialogue with expressive tones of voice. This association technique helps auditory right-brain learners learn how to learn languages and abstract subjects such as grammar, spelling, vocabulary, or algebra, traditionally taught in a left-brain way.

To remember procedures, auditory right-brain learners need to imagine each action as a movie in their heads, while discussing it aloud with sound effects or tones of voice, understanding the global overview first and then filling in the details. Their study partner should go over each step slowly and carefully with them, ask them to repeat the material back, including small, abstract words, and check their accuracy until they get it.

When writing, speaking, or reading they tend to get to the main point quickly and often leave out the unimportant, abstract words. When they express their thoughts, read, write, or spell, the right side of the brain, being global rather than sequential, does not attend to order and sometimes mixes up words, or in spelling mixes up letters. They may pop out with a word stored in memory close to the word they mean, for example, they mean to say dog, but instead say cat, because of their close association as four-legged animals. Also, they may read the first few letters of a word and intuitively try to figure out the rest of the word, thus coming out with a word that sounds close to the right one but is not correct. They get a global impression instead of reading each letter, in order.

When doing math, they understand the broad concepts or processes, but may not attend to the specific details of checking their work, doing step-by-step processes, or proving their answers. They can get an answer intuitively by finding relationships and patterns and grasping the whole process, but when it comes to the details of calculations, they may make errors. They may see a multiple-digit number simultaneously and come out with the first response that comes to mind. Thus, they may read 378 as 738 or 873. Others may mistakenly think they have dyslexia or a learning disability, but it is not— it is just that the right brain sees everything simultaneously instead of in linear order.

Since language in most people is usually located in the left hemisphere of the brain, auditory people with a right-brain preference may have difficulty with listening skills and may not be able to follow spoken language quickly. They often need directions repeated several times in order to grasp it and will ask those around them, "What did the speaker say? What are the directions?" Since they mostly grasp words that convey sensory stimuli, they may miss some important abstract words such as *not, if, after, before,* and other prepositional phrases. Thus, if they hear "Do not read this", they may pick up only "Do read this", causing them to make mistakes in school or on the job. Auditory right-brain learners need to learn some coping strategies. Those who are speaking to them should also understand that auditory right-brained people need instructions to be given slowly, one item at a time, often repeated two or three times, with sensory imagery, if possible. They need the extra milliseconds to take the words conveyed to the left side of their brain to cross over to be processed in the right side of the brain, converting each word into a sensory image, if possible with sound effects or tones of voice, and then, if a response is needed, to convert them back into words by processing them in the left side of the brain. This crossing back and forth between both hemispheres of the brain takes longer than it takes an auditory left-brain person, who hears words in the left side of the brain and formulates a response from the left side of the brain without any crossing over of the brain hemispheres. Because they are easily distracted by sounds, auditory right-brain learners need an environment in which only one auditory stimulus is going on at once, whether it is a person speaking or music. Headphones or earplugs are good ways for them to shut out unwanted sounds when they are learning.

Auditory right-brain learners think mostly intuitively, without words. They pick up meaning from music, sounds in the environment, and people's tones of voice. Left -brain people may marvel at how someone can think and learn without words, but it is a different kind of learning—it is an instantaneous knowledge that does not require words, like two friends knowing what the other is thinking without even talking.

To improve reading comprehension, right-brain auditory learners first need an overview of the reading material. Then, as they read, they can fit all details into the whole picture. They need to imagine the text as a movie with sound effects, accents and tones of voice, feelings, and music to make the material come alive.

They can read as if they were a movie sound effects person who must add the appropriate sounds and images to a script.

When they read, they grasp the key or main words, sensory words, words that sound good to them, or words for music or sounds. Vocabulary describing sound attracts their attention. Auditory right-brain learners comprehend better when they read aloud, or, if that is disruptive to others, they should read softly or hear the words in their head. As with listening, they tend to skip abstract words that do not invoke any imagery such as articles, connecting words, prepositions, time words, conditional words, and auxiliary verbs, or they tend to substitute these words for each other. Thus, they may tend to read quickly because they skip too many of these abstract words. Also, they may read the first few letters of a word and intuitively figure out the rest of the word, thus coming out with words that sound a little like the right word, but are missing the middle or ending syllable. The right hemisphere of the brain does not pay attention to reading each letter of the word in order, one at a time. It gets an impression of the word because it sees all the letters simultaneously and says the first word that pops out, be it right or wrong.

As they are better at grasping an overview, big picture, impression, or main idea of what they are reading, they tend to miss details that may affect the meaning. On reading comprehension tests, they get the gist of what they read, but have difficulty with specific facts about time order, sequence, or detail questions.

To overcome this right brain tendency, they need auditory right brain techniques to get them to slow down and consciously make an effort to pay attention to directionality, such as reading words in English from left to right, letter by letter, without skipping words. By using pointers, guides, or highlighters in color as they read aloud they can monitor their progress to ensure that they read each letter of a word, in order, without skipping parts of the word and that they read each word in a passage, without skipping any. Visualization techniques help them experience what they are reading, word by word, or phrase by phrase, like hearing the sound track of a movie to make sure they do not miss anything and to help improve retention of smaller details, abstract time words, and prepositions. (Note: Auditory right-brain people do not visualize as visual right-brain people do as they are not focusing on what things look like, but they are intuitively experiencing the text with the sounds that would accompany it as if a sound track to a movie.) They can talk about what they are experiencing in their head as they do this, either to someone else or to themselves, aloud, or hear the sounds of the words inside their head, as an auditory reinforcement to what they are imagining.

In the work force, you may find auditory right- brain people in jobs that require listening to sounds, music, and nature in a global, simultaneous way. They may be musicians, songwriters, musical arrangers, conductors, members of a rock group, jazz trio or quartet, rhythm and blues group, orchestra, or band.

Auditory right brain people are so sensitive to sound and its variations that they are the ones who make good sound mixers and sound editors for a recording studio, concert halls, or music, movie, video, or audio production company. Some may become the sound effects technician or special effects technician for a movie, television, video, or audio production company.

If they work in the fields of medicine, science, technology, social science, business, finance, education, service industries, marketing, sales, or professional services, they can learn their career or job through auditory right-brain techniques and will be contributors to making everything in their workplace sound good.

Whatever their profession is, auditory right-brain learners are low-key, laid back people who enjoy the harmony—and music, and the positive vibrations that flow from people around them.

Adapting Learning to an Auditory Right-Brain Style to Improve Memory

Auditory right-brain learners can ask instructors to enhance their lectures to aid in recall by giving the big picture or main idea first, before filling in with the details, and to use short sensory language, music, or sound effects along with images, mind maps, real-life objects, or demonstrations. Because many lectures are too fast-paced for them to follow while taking notes, they need to have a printed study guide, text, or tape recording so they can work at their own pace to convert the words into the following: a) a mental movie with images, sensory language, sound effects, and music along with their talking aloud or to themselves about what they are visualizing; b) illustrations of the information with key words highlighted in color as they talk aloud to someone else or themselves to associate the sounds of the words with the information; or c) mind maps or idea webs that show the main idea and details and their interconnections in colorful, creative ways.

They need to participate in real-life situations and find materials that give the overview or big picture using sensory words and visual aids that correspond to the subject, and work at their own pace converting it into a movie in their mind while talking about it with sound effects, rhythm, or musical tunes.

CHAPTER 14:
WHAT IS A TACTILE LEFT-BRAIN LEARNER AND HOW TO IMPROVE YOUR MEMORY QUICKLY?

What Is a Tactile Left-Brain Learner?

Tactile left-brain learners remember and learn best sequentially through the symbolic language of letters, numbers, and words. They also learn and recall using their hands and fingers, their sense of touch, and their feelings. They often hold a pen or pencil, and write to think and listen better. If they are told to put their pen away, they will find some other object to touch or something to do with their hands.

They are sensitive to language coupled with nonverbal communication such as a speaker's facial gestures, body-language, tones of voice, and mood, which makes them doubly aware of other people's messages. They maintain eye-contact mostly to read a speaker's expression and then look down and away when they think. They tend to be able to articulate their own feelings well and can easily empathize with others. They often gesticulate with their hands and are generally expressive. Tactile left-brain learners are sensitive to other people's feelings and their own feelings get hurt easily. They think with their heart and express their thoughts verbally or in writing in terms of feelings. If learning material is tied to a physical or emotional sensation it will be more meaningful to them. They spend time working out relationships, being with family and loved ones, writing heartfelt letters, emails, or texts, or talking on the phone to those who are important in their life.

Tactile left-brain learners get new ideas as intuitive feelings and then conceive of a step-by-step approach for carrying them out. When ideas come, tactile left-brain people feel impelled to write them down sequentially. They may wake up in the middle of the night with an idea and have to write it immediately. They can be passionate about their ideas, and this enthusiasm rubs off on others. They are highly motivated and use their logic and ability to express their feelings in words to convince others of their ideas.

How Tactile Right-Brain Learners Can Improve Memory to Learn Anything Quickly

Tactile left-brain learners can accelerate their memory and learning of anything quickly by participating in activities that require the use of their hands and fingers. They need to write what they see and hear in order to learn in a sequential way. They are interested in words or numbers. In seminars or lectures, they may take copious notes in a linear, sequential way, but they never need to look at them again. The act of writing or copying material from text or taking dictation from a lecture, by itself, helps their brain process information and enables them to recall it later. They also recall the order in which they wrote the notes.

Many think and listen better when they doodle, draw, or hold something in their hands. If restricted from writing in a seminar, you may see fidgety behaviors such as playing with objects, twirling pencils, tapping their fingers on their desk, or anything else they can do with their hands. Because of their left hemispheric preference, they tend to organize notes or make outlines, lists, diagrams, or charts.

For every subject they learn, they require active hands-on experiences with manipulatives or real-life objects to accompany a lecture or seminar. Once they have typed something, they will remember it. They also remember by constructing and building things with their hands in a linear, step-by-step way. In science, they need to not only perform the experiment (a good hands-on activity), but write about the results. They do not remember as well if a teacher just shows and explains new material to them without allowing them to first write it down or guiding them in performing a task so they get a feel for doing it.

In order to remember, tactile left-brain learners need to use paper, notepads, blank books, journals, diaries, stationery, electronic devices such as laptops, notebooks, or tablets; pencils, pens, a stylus for electronic devices, markers, crayons, paints, sculpting materials, arts and crafts, board games, computers, sports equipment that involves the hands, musical instruments, real-life objects, manipulatives, and other hands-on materials. Sequential computer programs that allow them to type, interact with others at a feeling level, and communicate with others are ideal. Communicating with others through social media sites on the Internet, emailing, or writing text messages or blogs, allows them to use their hands and involve their feelings.

When memorizing material for a test, they will best recall the material they learned by touching, writing, drawing, or experiencing it at an emotional level. They can recall a subject in detail when they can associate the experience with a physical sensation or involving their feelings while learning, which makes it more meaningful and relevant to them. They can learn from movies, DVDs, videos, or books that touch their emotions and heart. Visual and auditory details can be remembered if tied with an emotion. Thus, they will remember seeing a smile that conveys warm feelings and remember hearing words conveyed with love. When tactile children learn their language, it is the love of their parents expressed through words that helps the words sink in.

They learn well and remember better in a peaceful environment, such as a setting in which they can be surrounded by mountains, trees, or a lake. They need to be comfortable while studying. Since they are attuned to sensation on their skin such as hard and soft, hot and cold, rough and smooth, bodily comfort aids their ability to focus on learning. Thus, many like to stretch out on the floor, recline comfortably on a chair, or lie on a couch. They may be able to type, write, read or study with music, if it is music they like, because they focus on the feelings, not the words. The good feelings their favorite music brings help them tune out negative stimulus from others, focus on positive feelings, and stimulate them to be more productive.

They need positive feelings in order to concentrate or they may shut down. They cannot concentrate when they feel others do not like them. Negative vibrations from others, both verbal and nonverbal, need to be minimized. If they feel emotionally uncomfortable, tactile left-brain learners use language in an organized, clear way to question others about what they are really feeling based on their tones of voice, and will talk with others to straighten out the situation. If they cannot talk about their feelings, they can write them as poetry, essays, journal entries, or blog posts.

Tactile left-brain learners can benefit from learning in cooperative teams or groups, if they like the people. They thrive on positive feelings from group members with whom they feel comfortable, and whose appreciative words and warmth help them work better. If their socializing distracts others, tactile left-brain people can be encouraged instead to write to their friends in class. Writing about their feelings and socializing with others does not hinder their ability to listen and work, but actually increases interest in their work.

To improve memory of what they read, tactile left-brain learners need to internalize what is happening. They need to feel what the words describe and what the characters are feeling. They are bored if they cannot emotionally identify with what they are reading.

If they are reading about abstract subjects, they can personify the material, even if inanimate objects, to feel what is happening better. For example, if they are reading about a chemical reaction, they need to imagine themselves becoming one of the chemicals and experience themselves rising up as a gas. If they are reading a biography, they need to feel what the person would have lived through at a tactile and emotional level. They can actually recall everything they read if they convert into a feeling. What they do not convert into a feeling can be lost.

In whatever they read, they will also remember it better if they jot down their ideas as they read, in a sequential way. They may read books or novels that have depth, feeling, and a powerful message. They may read self-help and how-to books to solve a problem, to help them deal with feelings and relationships, or to learn something important for their jobs or life skills. They prefer it if these topics were written in a step-by-step, logical manner.

In the workforce, you may find tactile left-brain learners in jobs that require the use of their hands and fingers or involvement of their feelings that involve working in a step-by-step way. They tend to be structured and organized in their work.

If they go into fine arts, such as drawing, painting, or sculpting, they approach their work in a detailed way. When they draw, they tend to be good at copying what they see in detail and paying more attention to the technical aspects of the art, such as the mathematical nature of perspective or color mixing, etc. They may enter the commercial arts and do layout, design, fashion illustration, children's book illustrations, computer graphics, or advertising.

Some play instruments or write music and songs because these activities involve both their hands and fingers and the way the music touches their feelings.

Tactile left-brain learners may be involved in farming, gardening, landscaping, floral arranging, architecture, drafting, city planning, electrical engineering, designing electronic, technological or computer equipment, technical writing, construction, building, painting, plumbing, wallpapering, the restaurant business, or cooking. When doing arts and crafts, sewing, knitting, building models, woodworking, sculpting, basket-weaving, or making textiles, jewelry, or pottery they learn by reading the instructions and working in a step-by-step way. The can express their feelings through any of the communication arts from print media to film-making, photography, dance, and theater. Because they are so attuned to feelings they also make good actors and actresses.

As writers, tactile left-brainers produce narratives, essays, journalistic forms of writing like newspaper, magazine articles, newsletters, website content, blogs, advertising copy, biographies, history with a humanistic approach, how-to and self-help books, and educational, informational, or technical instructions or manuals to help people do their job better. They offer clear, practical, step-by-step solutions. If they write fiction, screenplays, poetry, or children's books, they tend to learn the formulas and rules for writing in those genres. They may be involved with digital or eBook publishing and doing their writing, artwork, and layout on a computer. If they give lectures or trainings, they first write out their speech in a structured outline, and then follow the outline. They prefer to make their presentations more interactive and make only limited use of power-point so they can make personal face-to-face connections with the attendees. They speak with passion and feeling, in a clear, logical way to get their ideas across and penetrate deep into the heart of audiences.

Many are involved in step-by-step sports that involve their hands, and learn by writing the instructions for how their body should move or the rules of the game. If someone is explaining a tennis stroke to them, they do better if they can take notes about it, think it through, feel themselves doing it first, perform it, and have a coach give feedback so they can adjust the stroke until they get it right.

Many tactile left-brain learners become involved in careers that deal with feelings, help people, or alleviate suffering, such as medicine, science, social work, education, psychology, relationship work, therapy, humanitarian projects, running social organizations or family shelters, ecology projects, helping the homeless, the needy, or orphans, or working for peace, and so on. Whatever their careers, they reach others' hearts by involving their feelings and touching them in a deep way.

Adapting Learning to a Tactile Left-Brain Learning Style to Improve Memory

Tactile left-brain learners should ask instructors to let them do note taking from a lecture or seminar or from printed outlines, study guides, or data presented in sequential order to remember better. For note taking sequential notes on their own, they need sequentially organized books and other written and audio-visual materials. They can talk to the instructor or co-workers about their need for positive communication and feedback. If there is no change in a negative environment, they can write their thoughts and feelings in a journal or talk to someone. They can also learn relaxation techniques and coping skills to deal with their sensitive feelings.

Chapter 15:
What is a Tactile Right-Brain Learner and How to Improve Your Memory Quickly?

What Is a Tactile Right-Brain Learner?

Tactile right-brain learners are sensitive people who tend to think globally. To improve memory to accelerate learning, tactile right-brain learners look at the big picture or overview and learn using their hands and fingers, their sense of touch, sensation on their skin, and their feelings. They use intuition, imagination, language that expresses feelings, and sensory words.

They are adept at reading nonverbal communication and express themselves in a nonverbal way by making facial gestures or sounds of pleasure and displeasure or by gesticulating. When they speak, they use strong feeling words. They are sensitive to other's feelings and their own are easily hurt. They are moved by sad or touching parts of movies and books.

Loving relationships are important to tactile right-brain learners because they need to feel good emotionally to function. They spend a great deal of time communicating, either by phone or face to face, so they can read other people's nonverbal expressions and tones of voice. Their eyes alternate between maintain eye contact mostly to read other's expressions and looking down and away to think.

Tactile right-brain learners think with their hearts and

express their thoughts nonverbally. They receive new ideas and information intuitively or through gut feelings, as if an entire thought package comes to them as a finished product along with a strong feeling about it. They feel passionately about these ideas and can be extremely persuasive in trying to motivate others as to their value. They may not be detailed or systematic in bringing the idea into reality but often jump in and carry it out impulsively. Having the end product in mind they will try to get there as quickly as possible without worrying about details.

Since they do not need to think in words, they can understand new information quickly because they can comprehend the whole picture instantaneously. They often startle those around them by accurately describing what the other person is thinking. They can get the gist of a two-hour lecture in moments through intuition.

Tactile right-brain learners work in an original and imaginative way. They often come up with new images and designs that no one has thought of before. As writers, they gravitate to imaginative kinds of writing. In the arts, they create new art forms or new ways of presenting old forms. They may use art to express their feelings. They may be involved with arts and crafts, painting, drawing, sculpting, sewing, knitting, textiles, pottery, basket-weaving, jewelry-making, or woodworking. Some like to play an instrument and create their own original and imaginative music and songs, filled with feeling. They can play by ear and pick out a tune without reading music.

Some tactile right-brain people enjoy games and sports that involve their hands. Since they do not have the patience for the constraint of organized games with long directions, rules and regulations, they prefer to play for fun. They do not necessarily play to win, but for the social contact with people they like, or because they like the feel of the game. When learning a new game, they tend to just jump in and perform it, getting a feel for it as they go along and learning by trial and error. Many prefer free-form games and sports involving tactile sensations in which they can be creative in their moves such as dance, gymnastics, ice skating, roller skating or Rollerblading, or swimming.

How Tactile Right-Brain Learners Can Improve Memory to Learn Anything Quickly

Tactile right-brain people can improve memory to accelerate their learning quickly by involving their hands, fingers, and feelings. Since they are not attuned to symbolic language, they learn and recall through sensory language or nonverbal communication that gives the big picture. They learn and remember by drawing pictures, diagrams, illustrations, maps, and making sculptures, models, or artistic booklets.

Tactile right-brain learners remember by note taking through drawing but never need to look at them again. They remember new material better when they do note taking using calligraphy or colorful, artistically drawn letters. The act of drawing or writing artistically helps them understand and remember the material. While listening to seminars, talking on the phone, or speaking to someone, they may doodle or jot down quick sketchy notes, pictorial icons, diagrams, or mind maps in a way that shows the interrelationships between the ideas. They tend to write or draw in a circular way all over the page in no particular order. Since they are not auditorially attuned to abstract language, it helps if they can see visuals or graphics to copy.

To listen, recall, or think better, they need to do or hold something with their hands. It could be a pen, paintbrush, clay, a computer mouse, or any object. If they are told not to touch anything, they will fidget by playing with objects, tapping their fingers on their desk, playing with their hair, or anything else they can do with their hands to help them listen.

They also need the big picture, not the small details, or they will feel lost. They may become impatient with lengthy written directions, and would rather just get a feel for the project at hand. When remembering how to do a math problem they need to see and draw or write out the whole problem with the answer and all the steps mapped out. Then, they should try to do it themselves. The right side of the brain is adept at figuring out mathematical patterns just from seeing the problem and its solution and similar examples several times.

When they need to use study skills and test- taking skills to memorize material for a test, tactile right- brain learners recall best that which they felt, touched, drew, wrote, or identified with at the level of their emotions. The subject matter or any auditory or visual material needs to be tied to their tactile sense and emotions.

Tactile right-brain people need hands-on experiences and manipulatives to learn. Lecturing or reading directions will not be as effective unless their hands can be involved. For example, writing and illustrating the table of elements can help them remember it. If it is not possible to use their hands, they need to use their imagination to visualize themselves doing the task with their hands and feeling the sensation in their mind.

The following materials help tactile right-brain people learn quickly: sketch pads, drawing paper, notepads, blank books, diaries, electronic devices on which to draw such as a laptop, tablet, or notebook, pencils, pens, markers, crayons, a stylus, sculpting tools, paints, and arts and crafts materials. In math, using objects, counters, calculators, or manipulatives help them learn faster. Real-life items, such as tools and equipment from all fields, board games, sports equipment, or musical instruments can help them learn many subjects. They like the more free-flowing, nonsequential aspect of the computer offered by the use of the mouse, or user- friendly programs that require a click on an icon. Their tactile dexterity can also make them quick at typing or texting. They may also be good at computer graphics.

Tactile right-brain learners remember best in a positive learning environment that is physically and emotionally comfortable. Negative nonverbal communications from others need to be eliminated. Due to their sensitivity to nonverbal communication, their right brain picks up sarcastic tones, resentment, hatred, annoyance, and other negative feelings. When they hear these tones, their openness to learn shuts down. They may withdraw or respond nonverbally, expressing resentment through defiant looks, resistant body language, and negative tones of voice. Their attentiveness increases when they are not distracted by the negative feelings from others.

Coaches or instructors can help them refine their technique if they offer help in a positive way when asked, but they need to be careful that the tactile right- brain person does not perceive any negative tones or they will turn off to them. It is better to wait until the tactile right-brain person asks for advice first before offering it, lest it be taken the wrong way.

Tactile right-brain learners like to work in a peaceful environment or a natural setting. They need to be comfortable while studying and will stretch out on the floor or in a chair, or lie on a couch. They can learn with or without music, but it has to be music they like or they will be disturbed. They are not distracted by music when they read or study because they do not focus on words; they get a wholistic impression of the music, its message and mood from the tune and the words combined, and pick up positive feelings. Some enjoy music that combines the sounds of nature with pleasant music. Music has a calming, relaxing influence, minimizes sad and negative feelings, lifts their spirits, and increases their memory and ability to learn.

Working in cooperative teams or with one or two people they enjoy can increase their ability to learn because they thrive on the positive feelings from others. Praise, appreciation, and positive nonverbal expression accelerate their learning.

To improve memory of what they read and increase reading comprehension, tactile right-brain learners need to feel nonverbally the written message or identify at a feeling level with the subject or character. They can thumb through a book, open a page, and find whatever information they need without reading all of it. They will often skip over details and lengthy explanations to get to the bottom line. Of course, this tendency is useful for fun reading, but for scoring well on a reading test for the ACT or SAT college entrance exam, college boards or certification exams, or on any test for a course or grade, they must use their tactile-right brain strategies to recall *every* word, as critical reading and close reading relies on that ability!

They like books that touch their emotions and become bored if they cannot relate to the emotional interaction between characters. When reading about abstract subjects they may personify and assign feelings to the material to make it come alive and remember it.

Books that are rich in imagination and have depth, feeling, or a powerful message appeal to them. They like how-to and self-help books dealing with feelings and relationships. After reading, they remember the text if they make sketches, drawings, or iconic symbols as they go along. When note taking they write key words, preferably in color or with an artistic design. Note taking in a pictorial or diagram form, such as a mind map, helps tactile right-brain learners remember them better.

In the workforce, they may be writers, artists, photographers, film-makers, dancers, or musicians. They may work in engineering, architecture, city planning, technical writing, designing electronic, technical or computer equipment, drafting, electrical work, construction, building, farming, gardening, landscaping, floral arranging, painting, plumbing, wall-papering, culinary arts, or any field involving their hands. They can find easier, more efficient, and more creative ways of doing these jobs and will look at them through a perspective that no one had thought of before.

Some may be involved with acting, often looking at life in new ways. If they go into acting they are good at portraying the feelings of other people. Their sensitivity to other people's feelings may involve tactile right-brain learners in professions that allow them to alleviate other people's suffering or help people such as social work, psychology, therapy, education, medicine, health, humanitarian projects, or working for peace.

Whatever field they go into, they will provide the feeling content, the imagination, the nonverbal connection between people, and move the hearts of others.

Adapting Learning to a Tactile Right-Brain Style to Improve Memory

Tactile right-brain people should ask instructors to provide the big picture or overview using short, sensory language to help them remember. They should be allowed to draw, do hands-on projects, or make a mind map in a global, creative, free-flowing way. Since it is hard for them to follow auditory presentations, when note taking or doing study or test taking skills, tactile right-brain learners need a written copy of the notes or readings complete with illustrations or photographs.

They should convert each word at their own pace into: a) a movie in their mind in which they relate the subject or characters with their own feelings; b) colorful, artistic, and creative drawings; c) mind maps showing the main topic and details and their interconnections; d) hands-on projects; or e) decorative and colorfully written words, calligraphy, or designs. They need to observe real-life demonstrations and draw a mind map that gives the big picture to improve their memory.

CHAPTER 16:
WHAT IS A KINESTHETIC LEFT-BRAIN LEARNER AND HOW TO IMPROVE YOUR MEMORY QUICKLY?

What Is a Kinesthetic Left-Brain Learner?

Kinesthetic left-brain learners remember and learn quickly and can improve reading comprehension and memory through movement and action of their body and large motor muscles in an organized, systematic way. Because the language function is in the left side of the brain, they can verbalize movement activities in systematic, structured ways.

Kinesthetic left-brain learners need to move a great deal and are restless when they have to stay in one place. If they are forced to stay in one seat too long, they will begin to move or rock in the seat, kick their legs, or get out of the seat spontaneously. Others may be distracted by their movements. Yet if they are given an opportunity to use their body, they will actually stick to a task with great concentration; it is when they are denied movement that they find some other outlet for their kinesthetic needs that may not be productive. They are going to move anyway, whether they are restricted or not—so at least their lessons should be structured in a way that includes movement as a positive part of their training.

They like team sports, organized games, or exercises that have rules and are done in a step-by-step way. Many kinesthetic left-brain people are extremely coordinated and can time their movements to be in synch with others. They may excel in synchronous swimming, gymnastics, acrobatics, or choreographed dance.

Not all kinesthetic left-brain people are athletic and coordinated, but they still require sequential movement activities in other fields, whether they are developing real estate, designing a software program or app, find a cure for a disease, or exploring a new hobby. Movement for them can be just mentally moving from one topic or project to another. They are systematic and orderly and tend to stick to and complete a task before moving on.

They need room to move around and comfortable sitting areas to stretch out and relax. If a place does not allow them to move about or has no action-oriented activity, kinesthetic left-brain people will feel uncomfortable and bored because there is nothing for them to do there.

They enjoy talking with other people while in motion or physically doing something, such as jogging, exercising, or working with someone else.

How Kinesthetic Left-Brain Learners Can Improve Memory to Learn Anything Quickly

Kinesthetic left-brain learners can improve their memory to learn quickly by using an organized, systematic, step-by-step approach that involves moving their bodies and muscles. They are language-oriented, so they can describe what they are doing and follow verbal systematic directions for movement activities. They can get on an exercise bike and read or study while pedaling, or walk around the room while memorizing the lines to a play. Learning games, simulations, role-playing and competitions are great ways for them to learn. Whatever movement they do, they prefer to use a formula, structure, or outline for their work.

It may appear to others that kinesthetic left-brain people are not listening because they are constantly moving, and they process thought better when their eyes are down and away from a speaker, but they are attentive when they are in motion. It is so stressful for them to sit still with their eyes on a speaker that they cannot concentrate on listening. Yet when they are moving about, they are relaxed, comfortable, and attentive.

Hands-on materials and manipulatives are important to kinesthetic learners, but they benefit more and recall better from moving their entire bodies, not just their hands. The simple act of standing up helps them recall and learn because it gets their legs, arms, and other muscles moving. To remember better, they need to write with large markers or chalk on a flip chart, white board, or chalkboard while standing. Doing math problems or outlining a report on a flip chart helps them to think and recall better. By writing in large letters on a whiteboard, they can involve their arm muscles and the activity into the kinesthetic realm. Kinesthetic left-brain people do not prefer to doodle or draw as tactile learners do, but they may do so only when it is the only movement they are permitted in a constrained work or learning situation. It offers them some movement of their arm and hands, which may not fully satisfy them but it is better than sitting still.

Whatever subject they learn, kinesthetic left- brain learners need to remember by doing something in a sequential way. Just listening to lectures and verbal explanations is not enough for them to assimilate and recall the material. They can benefit by volunteering to be a how-to demonstrator instead of just watching a demonstration. If they hear action words in sequential order, they will physically understand the material. They need a coach who will actively work through the steps of a process. If they are learning how to use a computer, they have to be at a computer while going through each step. If they are learning about carpentry, they will need the tools and materials so as the instructor models for them how to build something they can do it as they learn. They will remember not what an instructor does, but what *they* do.

When doing study skills or note taking to memorize material for a test or examination, they recall what they did with the material. For study skills, kinesthetic left-brain learners need to act out or dramatize the material, either physically or in their mind, so they can remember what their body did or what they imagined doing. If the subject is math or science, they need to work out the problems or experiments in a step- by-step way in real-life applications, for example, by doing the math required for sending a spaceship to the moon, mixing chemicals to produce medicine, or writing a software program. If circumstances do not allow a kinesthetic left-brain learner to do an activity, their next best resort is to watch activity movies on television or in a theater, using streaming video, or watching a program on the Internet or on any electronic device, preferably sequentially-presented programs.

Another kinesthetic method for them is to visualize themselves in their mind moving. In this way, they can experience the action within themselves without being noticeable to others. They should feel in their mind that their body is moving or enacting whatever it is they are trying to learn, even while their physical body remains still. This will also activate neuronal growth in their brain as if they had actually physically performed the action.

Kinesthetic left-brain learners thrive on achievement, winning, challenges, and discovery. Being goal-oriented, they enjoy the thrill of the game, and their motivation increases in a competitive environment. They like competing with themselves and beating their own record or against teams. Since the left side of the brain handles facts and figures, kinesthetic left-brainers tend to discuss game scores or keep records of achievement of others or themselves. Converting any learning experience into a competitive game helps kinesthetic left-brain people learn better.

Kinesthetic left-brain learners need manipulatives; organized games; building materials; sports equipment, such as balls, basketball hoops, jump ropes, and exercise bikes; science projects; large markers to write on large pieces of paper, flip charts, or white boards; computers; musical instruments; hands-on models; kits; or real objects to move. They like high action yet structured programs, games, and apps on the computer or any electronic digital device.

Kinesthetic left-brain learners can read, work, or study with or without music. Moving or dancing to the rhythm and beat of music can stimulate them to work better. When their muscles are in motion, stress is reduced, their attention and motivation increase, and they learn faster. Kinesthetic left-brain people enjoy playing musical instruments that engage the whole body. They can handle a systematic approach to learning an instrument and will attend to the technical aspects of playing, such as timing, rhythm, and reading music.

Working in cooperative groups or teams helps the kinesthetic left-brain learner because they can move around from group to group. They like to work from a plan or structured outline, so they know each step of the process beforehand. Interaction with different people in different groups fulfills their need to be where the action is.

To improve memory and reading comprehension to learn anything quickly, kinesthetic left-brain learners should get actively involved in the reading material, either by physically acting out the text or imaging themselves doing so. They should imagine experiencing their muscles moving by acting out in their mind what the words describe in sequential order. To engage their interest and remember what they read, kinesthetic left- brain learners need to convert the words into an action movie in their mind in which they are part of the action. They tend to forget whatever they do not imagine themselves doing in their mind as they read.

Kinesthetic left-brain learners prefer to read action-packed books. They like to read about movement- oriented activities in a detailed, step-by-step, well-organized way if it can help them improve what they do. The left brain's ability to think in terms of language helps them understand verbal or written directions for action-oriented subjects. They enjoy how-to books that help them perform better if written in logical, sequential ways. Business people enjoy reading how-to suggestions for improving their businesses. Sports lovers enjoy books that help them perfect their techniques.

Kinesthetic left-brain learners need a purpose and action-oriented reason to be motivated to read. If they know their sales will increase if they read the training manual, they will be sure to read it. If they know they need to pass the driver's license examination, they will force themselves to read the manual.

In the work place, kinesthetic left-brain people can be found in jobs that require movement along with left-brain organization, putting what they do into words, or giving detailed verbal directions to others. Jobs that require traveling, speaking, and being clear and organized in one's presentation are found in sales, marketing, district management, owning a self-employed business, teaching, and training. Kinesthetic left-brain people who go into the sciences may be involved in experiments, research and laboratory work, or medical fields, becoming doctors and nurses.

Since they excel at movement jobs that are related to being on time, a function of the left side of the brain, they may be pilots, train conductors, chauffeurs, truck drivers, delivery people, or parcel, express mail, or postal workers. Work that involves the physical body and using details, measurements, and precision are construction, engineering, roadwork, farming, painting, wallpapering, plumbing, electrical work, cleaning, furniture crafting, and doing repair work. Jobs that require physically protecting other people and that use the left-brain attention to structure, organization, and rules are in areas such as the armed forces, such as in the Army, the Navy, the Coast Guard, or the Marines, or in the police force, fire department, or secret service.

Kinesthetic left-brain learners may be involved in organized sports and games or may use their verbal abilities to become sportscasters or coaches and instructors in movement fields such as aerobics, exercise, or dance. They may write action stories, sports columns, reviews of movies, dance, or theatrical performances, or organized and structured how-to books. Their ability to visualize action on a screen or stage may make them good screenwriters and playwrights. As artists, they are structured and systematic in their work and will portray detailed action through illustrations, cartoons, comic strips, or commercials for advertising. They may be directors of movies, plays, or dance groups. They may become actors and actresses, musicians, performers, or instructors of performing arts that require body movement.

Adapting Learning to a Kinesthetic Left-Brain Style to Improve Memory

Kinesthetic left-brain learners should ask instructors to let them do movement activities in a sequential way to help them remember the material. If instruction is presented as a lecture, they need to ask for outlines or study guides or do their own note taking in sequential order, so they can convert the words into: a) actions; b) a movie in their mind in which they imagine themselves doing the action; or c) an outline while they stand up and write it in large size on a flip chart or white board. They can find sequential material, either written and in audio-visual format that relates to the subject and convert the text into a physical action or an imagined action in their mind.

CHAPTER 17:
WHAT IS A KINESTHETIC RIGHT-BRAIN LEARNER AND HOW TO IMPROVE YOUR MEMORY QUICKLY?

What Is a Kinesthetic Right-Brain Learner?

Kinesthetic right-brain learners can improve memory and reading comprehension to learn quickly through moving their gross motor muscles in a creative, imaginative, free-flowing, and unstructured way. They do not think or recall in words, but get information intuitively.

They become highly restless if forced to stay still or remain in one place too long. Kinesthetic left-brain learners will feel so constrained and physically stressed that they will start to move around anyway. Their need to keep moving and changing activities may make them look hyperactive to others. It is actually when they are denied movement that they look distracted. It is better to give them movement activities related to the learning task, such as learning games, exercises, or simulations.

They will then be able to concentrate as well as people of other styles do when working in their element. Unless given productive activities related to their work, they will kick or swing their legs under the table, drum on the tabletop, slouch, rock in their seats, or find excuses to get up, whether it is to get a snack or look out a window.

Not all kinesthetic right-brain learners are athletes. There are many other activities that involve movement. For them, movement can be moving in their mind from one topic or project to another.

Kinesthetic right-brain learners can think about several things simultaneously and can have many projects going on at once. They can keep each one straight in their minds without any difficulty. They work in an impulsive, quick way, wanting to see results immediately so they can move on to another activity. In the rush to complete a project, they may not worry about whether the parts were done to perfection. They see the whole picture, not the details.

There are times when they consider a job done just by having thought of it. Some kinesthetic right-brain people put the idea out, do some preliminary work, and move on to another project. It is up to the detail-oriented people around them to pick up the pieces and complete the task so they can then move on to create new inventions. They have a wealth of new ideas and discoveries, like a brainstorm session in motion, giving the world a seeming endless supply of novel, unique ideas.

Being goal-oriented, kinesthetic right-brain learners have the ability to get things done, handling many projects at once. They are not time-oriented, so they do not tend to stick to schedules, routines, or time constraints. They are go-with-the-flow people who will do what they feel like at the moment. They can keep work moving and be a wealth of creativity and imagination, although others have to be willing to accept their lack of consciousness of time. At work, as frequently as they arrive late, they may also become so absorbed in a task that they may stay overtime just to complete it, giving you more productivity than what you are paying them to do!

A kinesthetic right-brain learner needs a comfortable

environment, full of activity, with room to stretch out and move. Some will get up and leave if they are bored or in a restricted environment. Being outdoors is high on their list because there they can move freely.

Kinesthetic right-brain people enjoy being with other people when they can do something together that does not require a lot of talk. Watch them during a football game and you may hear grunts, moans, or cheers. They can communicate action without speaking and use their body and arms to dramatize or express what they want to describe. When they do talk, they use short action words and get to the point quickly.

How Kinesthetic Right-Brain Learners Can Improve Memory to Learn Anything Quickly

Kinesthetic right-brain people can improve memory to learn quickly by moving in an unstructured, imaginative, and free-flowing way. They need to use their bodies and muscles to learn. Thus, they can remember better while cycling on a stationary bike, memorizing material by jumping rope, simulating or role-playing a situation, performing experiments, or playing creative games.

Kinesthetic right-brain learners, often adventuresome and daring, enjoy challenges. This group just needs to jump in and do it. They pick up the how- to information by intuition or gut feelings and learn by trial and error, exploration, and discovery. They fully grasp the overall patterns of any situation and know what to do. Their excellent visual-spatial relations, intuition, and quick reflexes enable them to look at a problem, instantaneously judge a situation, and move accordingly, without words or written directions, to find the solution.

Kinesthetic right-brain learners do not require step-by-step, detailed instructions. They are whole-to- part learners who need to see the big picture or overview first and fill in the details later. For example, they will not give a detailed verbal account of a sports event—they will give the highlights and the winning score: the bottom line. If they see an entire math problem worked out with the answer and several examples, they can figure out how to solve similar problems.

Kinesthetic right-brain learners listen better to others while in motion, with their eyes focused down and away from the speaker. They remember more when they are in motion than when they are sitting still. When they are moving, they can relax, concentrate, and absorb information better.

They learn and remember better by standing up to work. Writing on a flip chart or whiteboard with large markers works better for them than writing while sitting. By involving their whole arm, legs, and body, they can put the activity into the kinesthetic realm. Making a mind map of material they need to know by using their whole arm to write provides more activity and helps them recall what they learned. They doodle not because of a tactile need to write but because it offers more movement than sitting still.

They need active real life or simulated experiences. For example, when learning about accounting they would prepare a budget for a real company or an imaginary one they created for this learning experience. If volunteers are needed for a demonstration, kinesthetic right-brain learners jump at a chance to get out of their seats and do something. If they are learning a dance, they will remember it not by watching someone else do it, but by doing it themselves. They need to immerse themselves fully in the experience in an unstructured way. Many of them do not want long explanations; they want to figure something out for themselves. They need teachers who will take on the role of a coach, use only key action words, and guide them if they ask for help.

If a situation does not permit the kinesthetic right-brain learner to do an activity, their next resort is to watch activity on television, DVDs, videos, or movies.

To remember what they learn, they need to act out the material or visualize themselves dramatizing it as if a movie were playing in their head. When they visualize, they need to feel the movement in their muscles. Their body may move and sway as they go through the movements in their mind. When they receive directions to drive to a friend's house, they experience themselves turning the car right or left, or whipping along the curve in the road in their mind.

Good learning materials for a kinesthetic right- brain learner are manipulatives, games, building materials, tools, sports equipment, balls, exercise bikes, large flip charts whiteboards, large markers, computers with action games, percussion instruments, guitars or organs, rhythmic music, hands-on models, or real objects to move. They like unstructured, nonsequential, high- action, fast-moving video games, apps, and interactive programs. If a computer program is too slow or too structured, they become bored. They prefer moving a mouse, joystick, or swiping their fingers across a screen rather than using keystrokes on a keyboard.

Competitions and challenges interest kinesthetic right-brain people, either in games or on the job. They may participate in contests that determine who can sell or produce the most. They are goal-oriented and enjoy the thrill of winning points for themselves or their team.

Make a game of anything and they will learn it.

Kinesthetic right-brain learners do better using note taking, study skills and test taking strategies by remembering what action they *did* while learning. For them to concentrate, distractions caused by the movement of others have to be eliminated. Working in a study carrel, using a divider, or facing a wall can keep them from noticing the movement of others, but they have to be comfortable while studying. Being stretched out on the floor or couch gives their muscles freedom of movement. They can work and study with or without music. Because they do not listen to the words, music does not interfere with their reading. The rhythm or beat stimulates their muscles to move or dance in time to the music. Their stress is reduced and their attention and motivation increases.

By working in cooperative groups, kinesthetic right-brain learners have an opportunity to move around more from group to group. They thrive on change and on interacting with different people to satisfy their need for action.

To improve memory and reading comprehension, kinesthetic right-brain learners need to convert words into a movie in which they are part of the action.

Imagining that they are the director of a movie and converting the book or script into action scenes, while describing the action that would appear on their movie screen, will make a book come alive for them. Whatever they do not feel themselves doing—or imagining they are doing—as they read will be lost to their memory.

They read for the main idea or big picture, skipping small details, and are impatient with too many words. Thus, they tend to miss reading comprehension questions that deal with details, time sequence, or abstract ideas. It is not that they cannot remember the details, but they need kinesthetic right-brain techniques to master them.

Kinesthetic right-brain learners prefer short or highly action-packed books or how-to books that help them perform better. Unlike their left-brain counterparts, they need diagrams, photographs, or illustrations. They do not like to read a book from cover to cover but tend to skip around, getting what they need from it. They may learn by just looking at the pictures, glancing at the captions, or flipping through the pages, catching stray sentences that may give them all they need to know about a topic. They have an intuitive sense that helps them find what they need.

Kinesthetic right-brain learners need to know the end product before they start. Thus, they need to know the reason they are reading something. They will be motivated if they feel it will help them do something better. Watch them zip through a book if they feel it will help them be the top in their field, boost their sales, or get a promotion. Books with summaries or key points at the beginning or end of the chapter help them find what is important and relevant to them.

In the workforce, kinesthetic right-brain people can be found in jobs that require movement and frequent change. They may not attend to details, but they will work quickly to get a job done rapidly. With this group, speed and completion takes priority over spending a great deal of time on detail, as long as the end product works.

As scientists, kinesthetic right-brain people enjoy inventing, doing research and laboratory work, or experimenting in the fields of paleontology, anthropology, quantum physics, or chemistry. If they go into medicine, they may run their own practices so they can have the freedom to set their own hours, or move from one patient to another in ten different rooms.

They may be involved in sports fields, as athletes, coaches, instructors, trainers, or owning a sports facility or team. They may be involved with dancing, gymnastics, golf, track, skiing, skating, swimming, sailing, snorkeling, surfing, biking, gymnastics, horseback riding, Rollerblading, karate, judo, horseback riding, or aerobics, and so on. They may play football, soccer, hockey, tennis, and basketball for fun, but may have to work harder to adjusting to being on an organized professional team because of the rigors of the schedule, discipline, and routine involved in that lifestyle.

They may enjoy the adventure and risks involved in police work, firefighting, the space program, or the Army, Navy, Marines, or Coast Guard. Many of them like to be self-employed so they do not have to follow someone else's schedule. They may run their own computer, construction, painting, wall papering, moving, lawn, maintenance, plumbing, electrical, or repair companies.

They can be involved in building, making, or fixing things such as cars, houses, boats, motorcycles, computers, appliances, machines, or furniture. They may do work that requires physical exertion such as construction, building bridges, or lifting boxes. Some work in jobs that require traveling, but with little talk.

Long-distance driving, flying, chauffeuring, making deliveries, and trucking may satisfy their need to move, if they are not constrained by time schedules.

Kinesthetic right-brain writers write short action stories that get to the point or how-to books that give key points without much detail. If they are artists, they like art requiring action—huge canvasses or sculptures with strong movement of color and design. They tend to make quick, impressionistic drawings that give a general idea of what they are trying to say. If they are actors or actresses, they may prefer parts with less talk and more action or be stunt people. If they are musicians, they enjoy playing instruments in which they can move their body. If they are singers, they prefer doing so with movement or dance. Kinesthetic right-brain learners tend to be better at playing by ear rather than reading notes. They also tend to be imaginative and can come up with new tunes or forms of music.

Their imagination, new ideas, openness to change, and inventiveness make them an excellent resource. Their commitment to doing makes them product oriented and able to produce a large amount of work in a short amount of time. As they move, the world also moves forward into new avenues and directions.

Adapting Learning to a Kinesthetic Right-Brain Style to Improve Memory

Kinesthetic right-brain learners need to ask instructor to provide the big picture or overview using short, sensory language and let them do kinesthetic activities in a global, creative, free-flowing way to help them remember better. Since it is hard for kinesthetic right-brain learners to follow auditory presentations, they need a written copy of the notes or readings or take dictation of a lecture and convert each word into: a) a movie in their mind in which they imagine and feel themselves acting out the parts; b) a drawing they make

155

with key words or numbers in colorful, artistic, and creative ways, while standing up at a white board or flip chart and writing with their large arm muscles; c) a mind map in color in which they show the main topic, the details, and their interconnections; or d) a kinesthetic project. They may need to find corresponding pictures, movies, or activities, in which they can participate in real-life demonstrations. They can convert information into a mind map that gives the big picture of the subject they are learning.

PART 5:
TO IMPROVE MEMORY USING YOUR SUPERLINK MEMORY AND LEARNING STYLE AND BRAIN STYLE

CHAPTER 18:

AN EASY 7-STEP PLAN FOR IMPROVING MEMORY QUICKLY

When you discover your best superlink memory and learning style and brain style, you are ready for this easy 7-step plan to apply this knowledge to remember anything quickly. You will be able to improve your memory through your brain's fastest superlink memory and learning style and brain style. You will discover the ingredients for remembering anything using your best superlink. The seven-step formula to rapid learning is:

Step 1: Know Your Brain Fastest Superlink to Memory: In the earlier part of the book, you discovered your brain's own unique fastest and best way of remembering to apply to any subject.

Step 2: Preparation and Planning: Next, you will plan your own program, beginning with the prelearning activities that will put you in the right frame of mind to remember quickly.

Step 3: Input: Then, you will find out what type of instruction, learning materials, and learning environment is needed to improve your memory.

Step 4: Reading and Listening Comprehension: Next, you will find out how to increase your memory of what you read and hear to improve reading and listening comprehension.

Step 5: Improve Your Memory: Then, you will learn how to improve your memory and retention to optimize learning.

Step 6: Note-taking, Study Skills, and Test-taking Skills: You will also learn how you can retain what you learned in your long term-memory by sharpening your note taking, test-taking skills, and study skills to improve your performance.

Step 7: Application: Finally, you will learn how to apply what you remember to your current situation.

The following section of the book is set up so that you can pick a subject you want to remember and use this guide to help you recall the subject quickly.

Depending on your superlinks memory and learning style and brain style, you can read silently or aloud, take notes, or do the activities suggested for each chapter with a subject you want to remember so that you will be doing the book, instead of just passively reading it.

Select a subject you want to remember right away. The subject can be a course you are currently taking or a self-study program. It could be a topic you wish to learn about on your own or one that you will need to pass a test or qualifying exam, such as a GRE, SAT, ACT, etc., or bar or medical examination. It can be a skill you want to remember, such as learning a computer software program, building a deck, or playing golf. Many of the activities in this book lend themselves well to courses that require reading a textbook or listening to oral presentations, but the process can be applied equally well to learning a vocation, craft, sport, hobby, or a skill required on your job. Even in a performance task you need to receive information from reading, listening, taking notes, doing something with your hands, or engaging your body. You will discover which memory method is the best for you no matter what area you wish to learn.

Thus, as you continue through this book, you will be learning two things:

1) how to remember anything quickly, and
2) the *subject* that you want to recall quickly. Once you master these techniques, you can use them for any subject or field you wish to remember throughout the rest of your life.

Exercise: Select the subject, topic, or skill you want to remember.

CHAPTER 19:

PREPARATION AND PLANNING FOR IMPROVING MEMORY QUICKLY

You are now ready to begin the process of improving your memory. The first steps are to ask yourself the following questions before you get started:

- What is my motivation, purpose, or goal for wanting to remember this subject?
- What do I already recall about this subject?
- What else do I need to remember about this subject?
- What is the best way for me to remember what I learn?
- How can I raise my self-esteem and use positive thinking about myself?
- What are some relaxation and stress reduction techniques to optimize my memory?
- How can I visualize success?

What Is My Motivation, Purpose, or Goal for Wanting to Remember This Subject?

People remember things that serve a purpose in their lives. Every day we are bombarded with information that we see, hear, smell, taste, or touch, but we only remember what we consider important; otherwise, we would be unable to sort through the multitude of stimuli we receive.

Our brain has the decision-making capacity to sort out

what is relevant. Whatever it decides to remember, it will remember. This is a choice we make continually and it is something we should keep in mind when it comes to learning. As information is conveyed to us, we can observe it passively and let it bounce off us, or we can take it in and retain it. Think about several subjects you have learned throughout your life. Were there times when you attended a lecture or read a book, hearing and seeing the words, but moments later the information was gone? You did not really *learn* the material— you did not commit it to memory. Were there other times when you decided that you really needed to remember the information you received so you paid close attention to it, absorbed it, and remembered it?

Somehow, you made a decision to remember it because you had an important reason for doing so, whether you wanted to excel at your job or you had an important test to pass. Whatever the reason, your learning increased because you had the motivation or a purpose for learning it.

Motivation to learn and remember is a key ingredient in presetting your mind for recall. If you take a few seconds at the start of any learning session and ask yourself, "What is my purpose or goal for remembering this material?" you will have programmed your mind to be attentive and interested. The more relevant the subject is to your life, the greater the chance you have for keeping your attention fully on the subject to remember it.

Determine why you need to remember the subject you selected and keep this goal in mind as you learn the new material.

Exercise: Write down your reason for wanting to remember the subject.

What Do I Already Recall About the Subject?

The next step in the planning stage of your learning is to evaluate what you already know and remember about the subject. To accelerate your learning, you will need to fit the instruction into the shortest possible time. One way to do that is to eliminate wasting time relearning what you already know. Time and life are too short to sit through the same material repeatedly. You want to focus on new information.

To make this evaluation, list what you already remember about the subject. Only write down what you are sure that you recall because you may need a refresher for some material. As you go through your learning program, you can skip or skim over what you already remember to save time.

Exercise: Write down what you already recall about the subject:

What Else Do I Need to Remember About This Subject?

After determining what you already remember, the next step is to evaluate what else you *need* to remember about the subject. Most people go blindly into a subject. They plod along from one point to the next, starting at the front cover of a book and ending at the back. If the book contains topics not relevant, you should skip them to avoid being slowed down.

If you take a course, then you will probably be guided by an instructor who will tell you what you need to remember. If you are doing a self-study program, you need to do some preparation in advance and find out what you want to recall about the subject. Do you want to master a certain process or skill and cover certain topics? Do you want to show proficiency in one area or know everything that was ever written about that subject? Decide what it is you need to remember to satisfy your goals. List those topics and use that list as your guide. In this way, you can select the most helpful material and skip what is irrelevant to your learning plan.

Exercise: Write down what else you need to remember about the subject.

What Is My Best Way to Remember?

Discovering your superlink memory and learning style and brain style is an important ingredient in the entire learning process. Using memory methods that are compatible with your superlink can be a key factor in determining how successfully and quickly you will remember the subject. By matching the right methods and materials to how your brain remembers, you accelerate learning by eliminating unnecessary barriers that can slow down learning.

Exercise: Review the information on your superlink memory and learning style and brain style described in this book and list the best memory methods and materials for you to learn.

How Can I Use Positive Thinking to Remember Anything Quickly and Raise My Confidence and Self- esteem?

If you had a hard time learning in school, you may not have enough confidence in yourself and your abilities. Perhaps you saw others earn high grades while you received low grades or even failed. This may have resulted in low self-esteem, negative thoughts about yourself, or thinking there is something wrong with you. Unfortunately, years of this kind of negative attitude may become a self-fulfilling prophecy. When we think we can't do something, we put so much energy into that negative thought that we may end up not succeeding. On the other hand, when we think we can succeed, we work with confidence and end up succeeding.

One study conducted by Harvard researchers, led by Robert Rosenthal, and that later became known as Pygmalion in the Classroom, focused on a group of ninety students of average ability. Three teachers to whom they were assigned in classes of thirty each were told that they were gifted students. The teachers, thinking that they had gifted students, taught them as if they *were* gifted and had high expectations of them. At the end of the study, the progress of each group was measured. The results were that the students met those expectations, did exceedingly well, and their achievement soared. (Canter, Lee, and Canter, Marlene. *The High Performing Teacher; Avoiding Burnout and Increasing Your Motivation*: A Publication of Lee Canter and Associates, Santa Monica, CA. 1994, pp. 25-26). What this study points out is that our performance can be influenced by our expectations of ourselves as well as others' expectations of us.

You might have been slowed down because you were not taught in your best memory and learning style and brain style. You learned quickly in the first few years of life because you were allowed to use your natural way of learning—the learning method that is easiest for you—which may have been any of the following: watching, listening, exploring, playing

167

learning games, hands-on learning, or any other method. But in traditional schools, students are usually taught in one or two ways, mostly by watching (a visual method) or listening to the teacher (an auditory one). If students do not have the same memory and learning style as the one used in the classroom they struggle to learn. During the time they spend trying to adapt to a memory and learning style that is not compatible with their own, the class has already moved on. These students do not know what is wrong with them or why others are getting it and they are not. They do not know that if they were taught in a memory and learning style and brain style that matched their own they would move along as quickly as some of the other students. But the students do not know what to ask for. They are prisoners of a system that is not working for them.

If you are one of those who experienced failure or felt you could not learn and remember as quickly as others, or were a good student and wanted to be better and could not, you were probably just as bright as those other children, but were limited by a learning and memory method that was not compatible with your own. The students who did well may have been those whose superlink memory style matched the teacher's presentation. If you were to take those who did well and put them in a learning environment that is not compatible with their memory and learning style, they also might struggle or find it harder to achieve.

How can we raise our self-esteem? First, realize that *every* human being has an amazing capacity to learn and remember. In the first seven years of life, children can memorize an entire language and the meaning of thousands of words. Our brain's memory does not shut down after first grade. There is nothing inherent in any of us that says that we suddenly become incapable of learning and remembering when we arrive at the doors of an elementary school. The same brain and memory that you used to assimilate an entire language in the first seven years of life is just as intelligent and prepared to learn after it begins school. To raise your self-esteem, realize that what happened to you in the past may not have been your fault. Had you been taught in your best memory and learning style and brain style you would have learned and remembered faster and more easily.

What is past is past and now you know how *you* need to remember. Start from today. Feel confident that you now have a memory approach that will work for you. As you begin to learn through the approach that matches your superlink memory and learning style and brain style, you will experience the feeling that others who have done so have experienced— you *can* do it. It is easy, fun, and natural. Having positive learning experiences will help you to start feeling good about yourself. Slowly, those feelings of past failures will fade.

You need to start a cycle of success. How is this done? Firstly, think of a time in which you succeeded at a task. It could have been a school subject, an extracurricular activity, or something you did on your own at home. Try to relive the experience in your mind. How did it feel to succeed? Did you feel happy, proud, and confident? Did you want to repeat the experience? Most people would say they would like to repeat the task because of the good feelings that accompanied the experience.

Now think of a time when you failed at something. It could have been a school subject, a sport or hobby, or something you did at home. How did you feel? Did you feel hurt, angry, frustrated, stupid, or hopeless? Did you want to repeat that task again? Most people, unless they wanted to repeat it just to prove to themselves they could do it, would say they did not want to repeat the task. Thus, because of the pain of the experience, they began to avoid the very area in which they may have needed to practice. The more they avoided practicing, the further they grew from mastering it. The cycle of failure began. The initial failure caused them to avoid the task, get further behind, and reinforced more failure.

It is time to break the cycle. By learning according to your best superlink memory and learning style and brain style, you will now find it easier to remember. Gain confidence. Start with some easy work to regain the good feelings that come with success. Then, as you find you can finally succeed, slowly add harder and more challenging material. Do not frustrate yourself by beginning with memorizing material that is too hard. Until you regain your self-esteem, master the technique of remembering in your best superlink memory and learning style using some review material. Then add new material as you regain confidence.

Whatever your level of education, know that you carry in your head a most remarkable computer. You just have to fit compatible software into the hardware of your brain for it to run properly. Many others who have tried these memory methods have succeeded, and you can, too!

Exercise: Tell yourself, I can raise my self-esteem and positive thoughts about myself by realizing the possible causes of my previous struggles with learning and memory. List subjects with which you previously had trouble, analyze how they were taught and how the methods may not have been compatible with your best memory and learning style. List methods from earlier parts of this book compatible with your superlink memory and learning style and brain style that could have been used to make those subjects easier to remember.

Why Are Relaxation and Stress Reduction Techniques Important to Optimize Memory?

Relaxation and stress reduction can improve memory. Medical research over the past decades has been exploring the connection between the mind and body. When we are in a state of fear or extreme stress, the body's survival reaction is to shut down our higher- level thinking portion and respond according to the part of the brain that deals with the fight or flight response. We respond with physiological reactions such as increases of adrenaline, rapid heartbeats, and constricted blood vessels. Your body is readying itself to run or fight, requiring the use of your arms and legs. During this state, you are not ready to remember a mathematical theorem or new vocabulary words.

People who had negative experiences of failure in the classroom enter this state of panic and fear when it comes to learning. Test taking may cause them to be fearful so they do not score well even if they studied.

Their teachers or parents may have been upset with them, inflicted physical, psychological, or emotional pain and punishment, called them demeaning names, or ostracized them because of their mistakes at school.

Years of reliving this trauma may cause people to enter a state of stress, panic, and fear when they have to remember something new. For successful learning to take place we need to learn how to relax and reduce stress. We have to program ourselves to break the cycle of failure and get out of the habit of fearing learning.

Relaxation and stress-reduction techniques can assist in the process by improving memory.

Step one is to put the past behind you and realize that these struggles with memory or test taking may not have been entirely your fault, and remind yourself that the fear response is only a habit. You now know what you need in order to remember; things *will* be different this time. By following a new approach that suits your memory style, you will be more successful. So, relax— this time you *will* succeed!

Step two is to get your body into a physiological state of relaxation. Our brain waves run at different frequencies. From thirteen to twenty Hz (Hertz) or cps (cycles per second) we are in the beta state, the state in which we function at work, driving, or in the fight–or– flight mode. From nine to twelve Hz we are in the alpha state, in which we are more relaxed, but alert. The alpha state is good for learning. The theta state, from five to eight Hz, is the meditation state. That is good for relaxation and stress reduction. From one to four Hz we are in the delta state, which is deep sleep. Before trying to remember material for the subject we are learning, we may want to reduce our stress and increase our relaxation by entering the theta state—the state of meditation. There are different ways to do this.

One way to reach the state of relaxation is to slow down our breathing. In fear, the hormones we release increase our heart rate. To reduce a rapid heart rate and to relax, find a place to sit in a relaxed position. Take some deep breaths, letting the air fill your lungs. Breathe to the count of four, hold for four, and release your breath in four. Do this slow breathing for several minutes, until you feel your heartbeat slow down. As you breathe in, feel relaxation enter you, filling your entire body. Imagine being filled with this relaxation. Feel your stress evaporate as calm and peace fill you. Imagine that relaxation opens you up to receive the wisdom and knowledge to help you learn and remember anything you want to know. You can then feel the stress of your body disappear and relaxation fill you.

Another way to get to the theta state is to still your mind and eliminate all thoughts of panic, worry, and fear. Sitting for a few minutes in meditation calms your mind. You can close your eyes in a relaxed manner. Concentrate as if you were watching a movie screen within. Sit in a relaxed manner, looking into the center of what is in front of you. Do not think about anything; just look into the middle of the field of vision. Your mind will become concentrated and focused. A feeling of relaxation will come over your body and mind. By keeping your attention on one point, you will find your powers of concentration become focused and sharp. You may feel a sense of peace. Some people even experience blissful joy. Your worries and fears melt away—you are now in the state where you are ready to remember whatever you want.

Some people try a variety of other techniques for relaxation. Some use music to get into this state. Early work with accelerated learning developed by the Bulgarian researcher Georgi Lozanov relied on music to get the mind ready for learning. Baroque music, which contains sixty beats per minute, supposedly synchronizes with the heartbeat, helping people get into an optimal learning state. Musician Steven Halpern has found that music with less than sixty beats per minute also works.

His research reveals that music with a slower beat slows the heart rate, putting the body and mind into a more relaxed state, ideal for learning. He has been a pioneer in producing music to accelerate learning. Some schools have used his music to create a calm, peaceful state in which students can learn with a stress-free attitude.

Some people like to do physical exercise or yoga to get the body relaxed. Exercise or physical yogas stimulates the flow of oxygen through the bloodstream, carrying it to the brain to eliminate mental stress and get the brain ready for learning and remembering. New research reveals that exercise stimulates the brain to make more connections that can increase learning and improve memory.

Whatever method you use, the end result is to calm the body and mind to keep them out of the fight-or- flight mode. Before beginning a memory session, spend five or ten minutes in any of the relaxation techniques.

You can do the same one every day, or you can vary them. Find those that work the best for you. The goal is to keep the higher-thinking functions in the brain open so that remembering the subject you want to learn can take place.

Exercise: Try different stress-reduction activities to find those that are best for you.

How Can I Visualize Success?

The last step in the planning stage for improving memory is to visualize success. New studies have shown that even thinking about doing a task results in neuron connections being made as if they had physically performed the activity.

This is a powerful discovery supported by scientific evidence indicating that by mentally going through a task, brain cells are forming connections for that task, accelerating our learning and improving our memory. Athletes have been using this technique for years. Before a competition, they visualize or imagine themselves winning. The power of positive mental mind-set and pre-setting brain connections for success is used in other fields as well. Medical researchers and doctors have reported cases in which after the visualization of good health, their patients' health improved. Health and wellness centers around the world have been established, devoted to helping people visualize themselves becoming healthy. The same technique has been used for increasing learning, reading and listening comprehension, and memory.

The technique is simple. Sit quietly in a relaxed state. You can get into a meditative state first so that the body and mind are calm and stilled. Select one of the following next steps based on your memory and learning style.

For Visual Learners: Picture yourself successfully completing the course in whatever subject you are trying to remember.

For Auditory Learners: Hear yourself say that you have successfully completed the course.

For Tactile Learners: Feel the joy of success of completing the course.

For Kinesthetic Learners: Experience yourself jumping up and giving a victory punch with your fist into the air and saying, "Yes!" after successfully completing the course.

Try to make the image of your successful moment as vivid as possible, using all your senses, with your superlink memory and learning style and brain style as the main modality. Imagine yourself being actively engaged in some action as a result of your successful learning. Live the successful moment as if it really has already happened. Repeat this activity daily. Know that you have already succeeded. Live each day as one more step leading to the success that is already yours. Students have successfully used this technique to win scholarships or admission into schools in which the competition was fierce.

Visualizing your success as well as doing the steps in this accelerated program of how to remember quickly to improve reading and listening comprehension, memory, study skills, note taking, and test-taking skills go hand in hand. The visualization of success adds the power of positive thinking to the memory tools you are learning. You are now ready to remember anything quickly the subject you have chosen to master.

Exercise: Visualize yourself succeeding at quickly remembering the subject you chose and write a description of what you visualized.

Chapter 20:
Choosing Your Best Instruction, Materials, and Learning Environment to Improve Memory Quickly

After preparing your mind for optimum learning, you are ready to begin taking in the information you need to learn quickly to improve memory. You will discover:

- how instruction should be delivered to fit your superlink memory and learning style and brain style;
- the learning materials you should use for your unique superlink memory style;
- the learning environment you need for your brain's fastest superlink memory style; and
- how to convert information from your weaker superlink memory and learning style to your best memory style.

You want to choose the type of instruction, learning materials, and learning environment that will allow you to absorb information that matches your superlink memory and learning style in order to remember anything quickly.

If you have control over your learning plan, you can make the above decisions about the type of information yourself. In many cases, though, you will be learning from others, such as through a course, a required manual, or a curriculum prescribed for your training in your field of work. Some of the above decisions may not rest in your hands but are left up to the instructor or the institution preparing your learning program. The people teaching you may not do so in a way that matches your best memory and learning style and brain style. In that case, you have two options. The first option is to explain to the instructor or coordinator of your studies how you remember best and ask him or her to present the material in a way that is compatible with your superlink memory and learning and brain style. The second option comes into play when the instructor or coordinator does not want to or cannot present the material in your best memory style. In that case, you need to learn how to convert the type of instruction to your own best memory and learning style and brain style. This chapter will teach you how to do this. This ability can be a powerful tool that will enable you to remember in *any* situation—you won't need to rely on others to determine whether or not you succeed.

Fit the Instruction and Materials to Your Superlink Memory and Learning Style and Brain Style

There are many ways to remember a subject. The medium of instruction and the materials are the communication methods used to convey the material.

Below are some of the different instructional media and materials.

Written material: books, eBooks, digital downloads, PDFs, textbooks, manuals, guidebooks, booklets, pamphlets, reference materials such as encyclopedias, almanacs, dictionaries, thesauruses, magazines, journals, newspaper, microfilm, microfiche, scripts, screenplays, poetry, charts, lists, diagrams, graphs, faxed material, emails, blogs, e-zine articles, Internet postings, websites, etc.

Graphic material: photographs, illustrations, pictures, drawings, maps, atlases, posters, cartoons, diagrams and charts with graphics, digital graphic downloads, graphic eBooks, PDFs, websites with graphics, illustrated apps, etc.

Audio-Visual Material: apps, digital audio downloads, streaming audio over the Internet, audiotapes, CDs, slides, power-point, filmstrips, DVDs, streaming videos, 3-D movies, radio, television, distance learning through teleconferencing, web conferences, web meetings, and webinars, cable television, educational television, and public broadcasting.

From Computers: information from the Internet, streaming video and audio, software programs, apps, virtual reality, webinars, web conferences, teleseminars, social media, e-mail, distance learning via computer, and on-line courses and degrees programs.

Hands-on Activities: writing, typing, drawing, sketching, painting, creating graphics on the computer, sculpture, building, constructing, arts and crafts, using tools, machinery, or equipment, role-playing, simulations, learning games, using manipulatives, dramatization, film-making, video production, theater productions, music productions, demonstrations, making discoveries, exploration, performing experiments, sports, exercises, etc.

Real-life Experiences: on-the-job training, fieldwork, trips to museums, learning centers (such as oceanariums, seaquariums, forest preserves, or environmental centers), or engaging in apprenticeships in stores or retail businesses, service industries, construction sites, hospitals, schools, factories, farms, delivery companies, airports, shipyards, railway stations, banks, the stock exchange, supermarkets, auto repair shops, art studios, theater or dance companies, concert halls, etc.), playing on sports teams (football, baseball, basketball, soccer, hockey, golf, etc.), or engage in training programs coordinated between places of employment and schools, etc.

Personal Instructors: direct instruction from teachers, professors, instructors, guides, mentors, life coaches, athletic or sports coaches, facilitators, trainers, skilled craftspeople, employers, managers, or supervisors. (The person may instruct through oral presentations or lectures, reading aloud material to the students or requiring students to read it themselves, providing printed graphic material, audio-visual material, and computer technology, setting up hands-on learning activities, or putting the learners into real-life situations in order to learn.)

Combinations of the above: Any of the above teaching methods can be combined.

Based on the description of your superlink that you read in the earlier part of this book, choose the instructional medium and materials from the above lists that corresponds with your Superlinks memory and learning style and brain style. For example, if you are a visual right-brain person, the medium and materials you need would be graphic material, movies, videos, printed material written in a visual right-brain style, or real life experiences.

If you can control your learning, then you can set it up in the way that will help you remember quickly. But we do not always have control over the way we are instructed. We may not be in charge of choosing the best medium or learning material, or selecting the learning environment. Is it hopeless? Absolutely not. What you can do is convert any instruction into your own best memory style. You can still recall the subject even if the medium, material, and environment do not suit your memory style. The following pages show you the instructional media compatible with your memory style and how to convert medium not in your style into your best superlink memory modality. Think of it as a translation system to show you what you can do to turn a poor situation into an optimal one.

The following information will enable you to convert a medium of instruction and materials or some aspect of them into the best medium of instruction and materials for your superlink memory style.

Converting Instruction and Materials into Your Superlink Memory and Learning Style and Brain Style to Improve Memory

Superlink: Visual Left-Brain Learners:
Media Type:
Written Material: Ideal for visual left-brain learners

181

Graphic Material: Label and describe graphic material.

Audio-Visual Material: Use a corresponding study guide or transcript or take notes to review later.

Computers: When graphics are the only displayed media, search for a corresponding online manual to read that explains the graphics, or do your own note taking.

Hands-On Activities: Read the directions for the activity or write your own.

Real-Life Experiences: Refer to a written description of the activity.

Learning from an Instructor: If the presentation is auditory, tactile, or kinesthetic, make your own outline, directions, or study guide to read and comprehend later.

Superlink: Visual Right-Brain Learners:
Media Type:
Written Material: Draw pictures or diagrams to accompany the text.

Graphic Material: This is ideal for visual right-brain learners.

Audio-Visual Material: For written text, or audio media without graphics, create your own sketches or graphic materials in color.

Computers: For programs with written text, draw your own illustrations, graphic images, or mind maps to accompany the text.

Hands-On Activities: Make an illustrated instruction booklet for the activity.

Real-Life Experiences: Take notes in color on the experience and illustrate them.

Learning from an Instructor: If the instruction is auditory, tactile, or kinesthetic, take notes by drawing sketches or graphic images of the material in color.

Superlink: Auditory Left-Brain Learners:
Media Type:
Written Material: Read the material aloud and discuss it.

Graphic Material: Talk about the material to yourself aloud or discuss it with others.

Audio-Visual Material: Ideal for auditory left- brain learners. For visual media without sound, talk about the material aloud to yourself or discuss with others.

Computers: Read aloud any text that appears on the screen or discuss it with others.

Hands-On Activities: Talk about the activities while doing them or create your own auditory step-by-step directions.

Real-Life Experiences: Talk about the activities while doing them or create your own auditory step-by-step directions.

Learning from an Instruction: For a visual tactile, or kinesthetic presentation, ask questions, discuss, orally describe the process, read aloud what you wrote, or verbally describe the moves step-by-step.

Superlink: Auditory Right-Brain Learners:
Media Type:
Written Material: Make an imaginary movie and hear the narration or dialogue spoken with expression, sound effects, or music to accompany the text, or invent rhymes, raps, songs, or rhythmic poetry about the material.

Graphic Material: Create rhymes, raps, songs, mnemonics, or poetry to help you remember the material; discuss the material with others, giving the global overview first.

Audio-Visual Material: If visual or auditory material is only the written or spoken word, add sound effects or read it with expression, while creating songs, rhymes, raps, or mnemonics to go with the material.

Computers: For materials with only written text or the spoken word, add sound effects or music, or read aloud with expression, using entertaining tones of voice.

Hands-On Activities: For visual, tactile, or kinesthetic activities, make a colorful mind map and add sound effects or music, or talk about it with others, using entertaining tones of voice.

Real-Life Experiences: For visual, tactile, or kinesthetic real-life experiences, make a colorful mind map and add sound effects or music, or talk about it with others, using entertaining tones of voice.

Learning from an Instruction: For a visual, tactile, or kinesthetic presentation, convert it into a movie in your mind, imagining the narration or dialogue with expressive tones of voice, sound effects, and/or music, and/or talk about it with others, using associations, mnemonics, poetry, raps, rhymes, or songs.

Superlink: Tactile Left-Brain Learners:
Media Type:
Written Material: Copy material or do note taking in your own hand or type it.

Graphic Material: Write a description of the graphics in your own hand, type it, do note taking, or make a model and label the components.

Audio-Visual Material: Do note taking and/or do the hands-on step-by-step process.

Computers: For graphics, write descriptions in your own hand, do note taking or type them out, or do the hands-on step-by-step process.

Hands-On Activities: This is ideal for tactile left-brain learners. Use a step-by-step approach and put it into words.

185

Real-Life Experiences: For visual, auditory, or kinesthetic activities, do note taking, and involve feelings.

Learning from an Instructor: For visual, auditory, or kinesthetic instruction, do note taking, perform hands-on activities, and involve your feelings.

Superlink: Tactile Right-Brain Learners:
Media Type:
Written Material: Draw, sketch, or make graphics, in color, to illustrate the words.

Graphic Material: Copy or draw the visuals or do a hands-on activity related to it; involve your feelings.

Audio-Visual Material: Draw, sketch, diagram, or make graphics, in color, or do a hands-on activity related to the audio-visual material.

Computers: Convert any written text from computers into graphics. If already in graphic form, copy it by drawing in color.

Hands-On Activities: This is ideal for tactile right-brain learners. Use a global approach beginning with the big picture or overview first.

Real-Life Experiences: Make color sketches or mind maps with illustrations to remind you of the experience.

Learning from an Instructor: Make sketches or colorful pictorial diagrams or mind maps of the presentation.

Superlink: Kinesthetic Left-Brain Learners:
Media Type:
Written Material: Act out the words in a step- by-step way or imagine the action in your mind, feeling it in your muscles.

Graphic Material: Physically act out the graphic representation or imagine the action in your mind in a step-by-step way, while feeling it in your muscles.

Audio-Visual Material: Dramatize or imagine acting out the action in your mind, feeling it in your muscles, in a step-by-step way.

Computers: Physically act out the written text or graphics shown on the computer, or imagine doing the action, while feeling it in your muscles, in a step-by-step way.

Hands-On Activities: Visual, auditory, or tactile activities need to be carried out physically, or imagine doing the action in your mind, feeling it in your muscles, in a step-by-step way.

Real-Life Experiences: Ideal for kinesthetic left-brain learners. Use as a step-by-step approach and put it into words.

Learning from an Instructor: For visual, auditory, or tactile presentations, carry them out physically or imagine the action in your mind, feeling it in your muscles, in a step-by-step way, putting in into words.

Superlink: Kinesthetic Right-Brain Learners:
Media Type:

Written Material: Physically act out the words or imagine doing the action in your mind, feeling it in your muscles.

Graphic Material: Physically act out the graphic representation or imagine doing the action in your mind, feeling it in your muscles.

Audio-Visual Material: Carry out the actions physically or imagine the action in your mind, while feeling it in your muscles.

Computers: Written text or graphics need to be physically carried out, or imagine the action in your mind, feeling it in your muscles, with freedom of movement and imagination.

Hands-On Activities: For visual, auditory, and tactile activities, participate in the experience physically or imagine doing the action, feeling it in your muscles, with freedom of movement and imagination.

Real-Life Experiences: This is ideal for kinesthetic right-brain learners. Use a global approach, beginning with the big picture, main idea, or overview.

Learning from an Instructor: For visual, auditory, or tactile instruction, physically act it out or imagine doing the action in your mind, while feeling it in your muscles, with freedom of movement and imagination.

In summary, each type of instruction and learning material can be made suitable for any type of learner.

There is no reason for books and graphic materials to be made only for visual people; books can be produced to appeal to auditory, tactile, and kinesthetic people who are either left brain or right brain or both. As a consultant and a writer of learning materials for many years, I have developed programs that deliver instruction through the medium that matches the learners' best superlink memory and learning style and brain style. For example, I created an entire pre-K, K-12, college and adult reading program, called Keys to Reading Success and Superlinks to Accelerated Learning with lessons in all eight superlink styles so everyone can improve memory to excel in reading, reading and listening comprehension, vocabulary, phonics, fluency, memory, note taking, study skills, and test-taking skills. Any medium can be converted to match the learner's memory style.

Exercise: Review the chapter on your superlink and then use the above information to find your best media of instruction and materials that matches your superlink memory style. Take notes of all the instructional methods and media materials that match your best memory and learning style and brain style to improve memory. Remember, if you are a combination of superlinks, select media materials from different parts of the above information, since you have two or more best superlink memory and learning styles and brain styles combinations.

The Learning Environment You Need

Your learning environment refers to where you will work, read, or study: the conditions in the room and other stimuli that can enhance or inhibit your ability to remember what you want to learn. You may have set yourself up with the right delivery of instruction and the right materials, but if your environment causes you discomfort or distractions, it will be harder to concentrate. To improve memory to accelerate learning, you want to eliminate as many steps that block your progress as possible.

'When you set up your own environment, you can control your circumstances. But when you are in a training or class situation, you may not have control over your environment. Thus, you may have to ask the instructor for some assistance in making some adjustments in the environment, or use coping techniques to help you adapt to the situation.

Below is a list summarizing the best learning environment to improve memory for each superlink, followed by coping skills for adapting a noncompatible environment into one that is compatible for you.

Superlink: Visual Left-Brain Learners:
Best Learning Environment:
Written material and the speaker are clearly visible.

- No visual clutter or disorganization. Printed material is neat and free of errors.
- Can work with or without music or auditory
- Distractions because they can tune it out.
- Room is complete with filing systems, visual organizers, time schedules, calendars, and clocks.
- The instructor arrives on time and finishes on time.

Coping Strategies to Adapt a Noncompatible Environment:
- Try to sit close to the front to see posted visual materials.
- Keep your own area neat and organized.
- Offer to clean up, organize, and decorate the rest of the room.
- Correct errors in printed material.
- Request a time schedule. Wear a watch. Offer to be a timekeeper.

Superlink: Visual Right-Brain Learners:
Best Learning Environment:
- Graphic or written material and the speaker are clearly visible.
- Visually attractive, colorful, and creative environments.
- Can work with or without music or auditory distractions because they can tune it out.
- Flexible schedule allows you to come and go at varying times.

Coping Strategies to Adapt a Noncompatible Environment:
- Sit near the front to see posted visual graphic materials.
- Keep your own area colorful, well designed, and attractive.
- Offer to decorate the area of the room at which you have to look.
- Use a color-coded, decorative calendar to artistically track your deadlines. Put up sticky-note messages to attract your attention and remind you of deadlines and due dates.

Superlink: Auditory Left-Brain Learners:
Best Learning Environment:

- You can listen to others and discuss your own ideas.
- Only one auditory stimulus at a time.
- No music in the background while studying or reading.
- Silence for reading or studying.
- Orderly environment has filing systems, organizers, and time schedules.
- Instructor gives out schedules. Comes on time and finishes on time.

Coping Strategies to Adapt a Noncompatible Environment:

- Sit with someone who will discuss the topic with you.
- Sit where you can hear the speaker well. Stay away from areas with noise distraction.
- Bring headphones or earplugs to tune out music or distracting sounds when reading or studying.
- If you need to talk to yourself or read aloud, sit in an area where you will not disturb others. (Most likely the only ones who will be disturbed are other auditory people.)
- Ask for a time schedule. Wear a watch. Offer to be a timekeeper.

Superlink: Auditory Right-Brain Learners:
Best Learning Environment:

- The sounds in the environment are pleasant.
- Sounds are harmonious with one another, for example, music combined with natural sounds.
- Talk is kept to a minimum, with key points emphasized.

- Flexible time schedule.
- Speaker is clearly audible and speaks with good expression.
- Absolute quiet for studying.
- No music in the background while studying or reading.

Coping Strategies to Adapt a Noncompatible Environment:

- Listen to music while doing work that does not require abstract thinking in the form of words.
- Sit where you can hear the speaker clearly. Avoid areas with noise distraction.
- Sit with someone who can repeat key points and verbal directions slowly and repeatedly, if needed, until you understand them.
- Bring headphones or earplugs to tune out distractions.
- If you need to talk to yourself, read aloud, or make your own sound effects, sit in an area where you will not disturb others. (Most likely the only ones who will be disturbed are other auditory people.)

Superlink: Tactile Left-Brain Learners:
Best Learning Environment:

- Environment is physically and emotionally comfortable.
- You can sit next to people you like.
- You know the schedule and a clock is available.
- Room is organized and neat, where you can easily grab what you need.
- You are permitted to write, draw, and doodle as you listen or read.

- Can work with or without music you like. Instructor has a positive communication style, using praise and positive words and positive nonverbal communication.

Coping Strategies to Adapt a Noncompatible Environment:
- Sit in a comfortable seat or bring a cushion or pillow to make uncomfortable seats feel better.
- If you do not like air-conditioning or heat, sit far from the ventilators or blowers.
- If you do not like sun glare, avoid sitting in the line of sunlight.
- If you like sun, or need a view of greenery or a peaceful setting, sit near the window.
- Select a location where you feel emotionally comfortable. Sit near people you like.
- Ask for a time schedule. Wear a watch. Keep an organizer for your papers.
- Keep notepaper and pens available. Sit where doodling, writing, or touching objects does not bother the instructor or others.
- If you need music where you like to work, bring headphones so as not to disturb others.

Superlink: Tactile Right-Brain Learners:
Best Learning Environment:
- Use comfortable seats. (Some may like to stretch out on the floor or couch, sit on a desktop, or recline or stretch out in their seats.)
- Physically and emotionally comfortable environment.
- You can sit near people you like and stay far away from people who you think do not like you.

- You are allowed to doodle, draw, or sketch.
- You can work with or without music, but it needs to be music you like.
- Flexible schedule.
- Instructor is someone you like and admire.

Coping Strategies to Adapt a Noncompatible Environment:

- Select your own seating to be physically or emotionally comfortable. Bring a pillow or cushion if the seat is uncomfortable.
- If you like scenery, sit near a window. Sit near or away from heaters, air-conditioners, or sun-glare, if they make you uncomfortable, depending on your comfort level.
- Sit near someone you like. Avoid sitting near people who make you feel uncomfortable or upset.
- Keep drawing paper, colored pens, or markers for doodling and sketching, and sit where this does not distract others.
- If you like music to keep you feeling relaxed and positive, bring headphones so as to listen and not disturb others.
- Keep a color-coded calendar or use sticky-notes as reminder of time.
- Keep objects or belongings that make you feel good to touch on your desk or table. Give your desk or area a personal touch.

Superlink: Kinesthetic Left-Brain Learners:
Best Learning Environment:

- Plenty of space to stretch out and move around. You can get out of your seat or work standing up. Comfortable seats.
- White boards or flip charts allow you to stand up and write.
- Neat, organized surroundings. Time schedules.

- Sit near the back of the room so you can move around without distracting anyone.
- If you have to sit to work, use a chair in which you can lean back, stretch out, wiggle, or move a lot.
- Ask for a time schedule. Wear a watch.
- Bring a challenging game or activity or something to do quietly at your seat if you get bored after finishing work earlier than others and have to wait for the next part of the lesson.
- If you like music, bring headphones so as not to disturb others.
- Do arm or leg exercises at your seat if you get bored or restless.
- When studying, stay in a study carrel, or put up a book or divider to block out the distraction of others' movements, or face a wall.

Superlink: Kinesthetic Right-Brain Learners:
Best Learning Environment:

- Enough space to move around and stretch out. You can get out of your seat or work standing up.

- Room has comfortable places to stretch out on the floor or couch, and if sitting is required, use chairs on which you can lean back, stretch your legs, wiggle, or move.
- You can play learning or movement games.
- You are permitted to work with or without music.
- When studying, sit at a study carrel, or have a divider to block out the view of others' movements and activities.
- White boards, flip charts, or smart boards allow you to stand up and write.
- Flexible time schedule, and if work is done, are allowed to leave early or keep working, if you want, well past the finishing time.
- Competitions, rewards, and awards for achieving a goal.

Coping Strategies to Adapt a Noncompatible Environment:
- Select a place where you can move around without disturbing others, preferably at the back of the room.
- Make sure if you have to sit, the seat allows you to lean back, stretch your legs, wiggle and move around.
- Bring a challenging game or activity, or something to do quietly when bored while waiting for the next task if you finish before the others.
- If you like music while learning, listen using headphones so as not to disturb others.
- Work at a study carrel or use a book or divider to block out distractions from others' movements or actions.
- Keep a color-coded calendar or use sticky-notes as reminders of time schedules.

Exercise: Use some of the above suggestions for your superlink memory and learning style and brain style and apply them to remembering any subject quickly.

CHAPTER 21:

HOW TO LEARN TO IMPROVE MEMORY USING YOUR SUPERLINKS MEMORY AND LEARNING STYLE AND BRAIN STYLE

Did you know that you could improve and increase your memory by using your superlink memory and learning style and brain style? A good memory is not something that some people are born with and some lack. Memory *can* be developed by anyone. The only difference between someone with a good memory and someone with a poor one is training. This chapter provides a practical, quick, and easy-to-use guide of strategies and techniques to improving your memory using your superlink memory and learning style and brain style to accelerate your learning.

Training Your Memory

We have a tremendous amount of data stored in our brain that we can pull up at will. One reason we do not remember certain things is that we did not make an *effort* to remember them longer for an extended period of time. Consciously or unconsciously, we *chose* to remember those items we do remember. If we want to improve our memory, we can do so by training ourselves to remember what we want when we want.

When we talk of remembering anything quickly, we want to learn the subject as well as recall it for more than just a moment. Sadly, when many instructors teach a subject, the students know it only until they are tested on it. Give them a surprise test a month or two later and all that hard work to remember the subject seems to have been for naught. How is it possible that we can spend six months to a year taking a course and forget what we learned years later? It is not that we do not have a good memory—we just do not have a *trained* memory.

Accelerated learning involves training our memory using our superlink memory and learning style and brain style.

Long-term and Short-term Memory

We have two memory systems: short-term and long-term memory.

Short-term memory holds something temporarily in our mind until we decide what to do with it. Consciously or unconsciously, we can either decide to store it in our long-term memory or dismiss it as something unimportant. Our short-term memory is a revolving door with new information entering continually. It can be compared to a computer screen memory. Information stays there as long as we are focusing on it and working with it. Then we must decide whether to save it in the hard drive—the computer's long-term memory—or let it be erased when we turn the computer off.

Long-term memory permanently holds something in our memory. There are many things we learned in childhood that were placed in our long-term memory that we have not forgotten: walking; riding a bicycle, speaking our language; writing the alphabet, or childhood songs and nursery rhymes;

among other things. These memories become a part of our database from which we can draw at any time.

Keys to Improving Your Memory

The basics of having a good memory are simple and can be learned by people of any age, including young children. You *can* improve your memory.

Step 1) Having a purpose or goal for remembering what you are learning.

Step 2) Consciously deciding to put what you learn into long-term memory.

Step 3) Use your superlink memory and learning style and brain style to store what you learn in your long-term memory.

Step 4) Keeping your memory active by retrieving it and using it.

Step 1: Having a Purpose or Goal for Remembering What You Are Learning

We are bombarded with millions of bits of information daily. With the opening of the Internet, the information superhighway, we have access to a huge amount of information circulating in the world on a daily basis. If we were to recall every single sensory impression and bit of information we receive we would be so overwhelmed we would not be able to focus on the range of activities that were more important to our lives. Life is too short to learn everything about everything; we must make a conscious choice about what we want to remember. This process involves deciding why we need to learn something. When we want to learn something, we must also decide why it is important for us to learn it. If we keep that goal in mind, we will put our brain on notice that this is material we *want* to remember.

Why did you remember your name as a child? When you figured out that people kept asking you your name, you decided that next time they asked you had better know it or they may think there is something wrong with you. Why did you learn those twenty-six meaningless sounds called the alphabet when you were just a toddler? You had no idea what they stood for or what words they went with, but you learned how to repeat these twenty-six sounds that might well have been nonsense to you. Why did you learn it? Maybe you figured out that your parents would show you off to their friends by having you repeat the alphabet and would give you that big smile and hug that you loved. Or maybe you surmised that your relatives would give you a monetary award for being such a good and smart child for saying your ABCs. You had a purpose for learning that information at age two, three, or four, which had nothing to do with getting a high school diploma. You could have just as easily been taught the ABCs in a foreign language, or the periodic table of the elements, or the names of all the bones of the body. We learned what we did because someone valued it, rewarded us for knowing it with either verbal or nonverbal gestures or material gifts, and this made us feel good.

The same principle holds true today when it comes to learning and remembering. You really wanted to learn how to drive so you mastered the physical act of driving along with memorizing the driver's education manual with all its facts, figures, and state laws. The same people who cannot pass a social studies test can pass a written driving examination on technical information and legal terms. Why? They wanted to remember the driver's education manual because it meant if they could learn how to drive they could have wheels. It is the same brain that is reading that driver's education manual that is reading other textbooks. Is there a selective gene in our body that discriminates between remembering a driver's education manual and a political science course? Not at all. It is our intention and desire to recall something that determines what we will remember and what we will forget.

Some possible reasons, purposes, or goals for remembering information or a subject are: to get a job or advance in our career; to improve our skills; to raise our salary; to get a promotion; to become certified in a field; to pass a test; to keep up with new knowledge; to help others; for enjoyment, personal growth, or curiosity; or for many other reasons.

Exercise: Take the subject you chose to study as you worked through this book and write a sentence or two stating why you want to remember more about this subject.

Step 2) Consciously Decide to Put What You Learn into Long-Term Memory

We must program our minds to send information into our long-term memory if we wish to retain it.

Otherwise, we will get the information, comprehend it, but it will be erased shortly afterwards. If we want to recall it for the long haul, we have to establish the reason for wanting to put it into long-term memory and the length of time we want it to stay in memory. Many people find they lack study skills and test-taking skills because they cannot remember what they read, hear, or study long enough to pass a test. That is because they do not program themselves to recall everything they learn for the entire duration of the course of study.

Here are some things to think about when you are trying to commit what you want to learn to long-term memory:

If you learn it the first time you read or hear it you won't have to go over the material again and again, wasting precious time.

You can use what you learn to work towards your job promotion, advancement, or passing a test, certification exam, or course faster.

You will have more free time to do other things.

You will be able to use the information right away. Decide that you want to commit what you learn to your long-term memory, the length of time you want to retain it, and why it is important for you to learn it.

Exercise: Using the subject you selected to learn as you work through this book, write your reasons for putting what you learn about the subject into long- term memory.

Step 3: Use Your Superlink Memory Learning Style and Brain Style to Store What You Learn in Your Long-Term Memory

This is the key to the entire process. I developed this technique as an extension of the application of superlinks memory and learning styles and brain styles. It works so incredibly quickly that everyone who has used it is amazed at how sharp his or her memory becomes.

The secret is: The key to improving your memory and remembering what you learn is to store it according to your best superlink memory learning style and brain style.

If you are visual learner, you have an excellent memory for visual detail. If you are auditory learner, you have a sharp memory when it comes to auditory detail. If you are tactile learner, you remember best what you do with your hands and fingers or what you feel, either physically or emotionally. If you are a kinesthetic learner, you remember best what you do and how your body moves.

I have developed a memory technique for which I coined the term, Virtual Reality Reading, or experiential reading comprehension. As you read or listen, convert the information into an experience in your mind that matches your superlink memory and learning style and brain style.

Visual people would *see* what they read and heard as a movie in their minds.

Auditory people would *hear* what they read and heard as the sound track to a movie in their minds complete with words, music, or sound effects.

Tactile people would *experience* or *feel* the sensations and feelings as in a movie in their minds.

Kinesthetic people would *act out* the actions and events of the movie in their minds.

By experiencing what you read or hear using your superlink memory and learning style and brain style, you are causing your mind to think an event is really happening to you. You have involved yourself into a true virtual reality experience that is taking place inside your mind through your best sense, supported by the other senses.

Books or lectures are real events that have been converted into words for the benefit of those who were not there. Writing is like creating a cyberworld in which reality is encoded into words, and reading decodes or converts it back into experiences and events. Reading is like cracking a code so we can recreate the writer or speaker's experience in our minds. The more vividly we do this and the more we involve ourselves in the action, the more we will experience being there and the more thoroughly we will remember it.

In this chapter you will learn techniques to help you remember everything you read in using a memory technique I developed which I call virtual reality reading with experiential comprehension to match your superlink memory and learning style and brain style. This method will increase your memory of what you read. You can use the sample reading passage below as a demonstration or select one of your own. The optional passage you can use for reading comprehension and memory practice is given below in Exercise 1. As you read, make a commitment to put this information into long-term memory. Attempt to remember *all* the details of this passage, including names, dates, and other factual information. Read it according to your superlink memory and learning style and brain style. Convert it into a movie in your mind, either seeing it, hearing it, feeling it, or doing the actions involved. Make associations for words, numbers, and dates, finding similar words or images already in your mind.

After reading the passage, cover it up and discover how much of it you remember now that you have experienced it as an actual event. If you imagined the story in your best superlink memory learning style and brain style, you should have found that you can answer every question and recall every detail after converting it into a movie scene based on your preferred sense. If you missed any questions or details, analyze why. Most likely you did not make a strong enough experience in your mind or you skipped over part of the text without imagining it. It is always fascinating to find that any text that someone did not imagine as a movie in their best superlink memory style is gone from his or her memory when he or she tries to answer the questions, while the material that the person *did* imagine in his or her superlink memory style pops out as if he or she really experienced the event.

You can do this kind of reading with everything you read, fiction or nonfiction, including informational texts. You can try this with reading the daily news whether printed in a newspaper or Internet news site, magazine or e-zine articles, trade journals, memos, newsletters, interoffice communications, text messages, E-mail, faxes, flogs, social media sites, or websites. The same memory technique can work with a novel as well as with scientific material, technical reading, history, the social sciences, health, medical books, training materials for any field, and textbooks on any subjects, or anything else you can think of. You can also use it for listening comprehension when listening to lectures. Auditory left-brain people can mentally record material directly in their minds, while those with other superlinks memory and learning styles and brain styles can take dictation so they can convert the material into an experiential event later at their own pace in their own quickest way of remembering.

Anyone can train themselves to read or listen to any material and put it into long-term memory. What does it take? All you have to do is be mentally present as you read. The moment you just look at the words without converting them, you have actually stopped remembering what you are reading. Remembering what you read only takes place when the words become images or experiences in your mind. Unless you are an auditory left-brain person who gets meaning directly from words, without converting them into corresponding experiences in your superlink memory and learning style and brain style, just reading (for other learning styles) word, word, word, word continually without images is not only NOT READING, it is a boring, useless task that does not help you. Begin to monitor your reading by making sure you are converting every word you read into experiences. Remember, the moment you stop making movie scenes in your superlink memory and learning style and brain style, you have stopped reading. You have begun to daydream or mentally wander. Every word you may have looked at or even said aloud while your mind wandered is gone from your memory because you were not really mentally present. You will then need to return to the last set of words that you imaged and reread that section using the virtual reality reading or experiential reading comprehension technique or it may be lost.

If you are reading to remember, you will soon realize that when you do not image the text as you read, you are wasting precious time. Not only do you *not* comprehend the information, you will not be sending it into long-term memory. That is why you may have had to read the same material over and over in the past. But if you are in a hurry and want to remember anything quickly, you need to read and remember it correctly the first time around. You will find that with a little practice you can have total recall and memory of everything you read. Just be attentive, do the conversion process in your best memory and learning style and brain style, and with hardly any effort, the whole passage will come back to you hours, days, or even weeks later because you transformed it into an experience that happened to you.

This method of reading comprehension and memory that I developed and tested with people of all ages is a powerful tool you acquire to speed up your reading, recall, and learning.

As you answered the reading comprehension questions for the sample passage, you may have noticed that as certain key words in the questions came up, an image or memory arose in your mind. If you are not auditory and you tried to remember the words, you may have drawn a blank. But if you instead ask yourself, "What did I experience in my movie?" while you were in a relaxed mental state, the movie would have rerun in your head and the answer would have appeared. You were using both your right and left hemisphere of the brain in this process. The image appears in the side of the brain that can picture it (usually the right side of the brain), and the word for it is recalled from your speech and language centers in the brain (usually the left side of the brain, although some people have some language in the right side of the brain). Thus, you have engaged your whole brain in this process. This kind of reading comprehension and memory is a great exercise for developing your whole brain. You are making more connections between the two halves of the brain and developing your thinking and memory powers as well.

Memory Improvement:

Exercise 1: You can use this sample passage to further practice the experiential virtual reality reading comprehension and memory technique in your Superlinks memory and learning style and brain style, or, if you grasp how it works, you can move on to Exercise 2 to practice it with an actual subject you want to read or remember.

Next, I will model for you how we can work together through the following sample practice reading comprehension and memory passage, Dave, making a commitment in our minds that we want to put this information into long-term memory. The task is to attempt to remember *all* the details of this passage, including names, dates, and other factual details. We are going to read it according to our superlink memory and learning style and brain style. I am going to involve both sides of your brain, the right and left side, for this exercise to show you how you can remember both the big picture and graphic images (right-brain functions) as well as every detail and the words for the experience (left-brain functions). Thus, we are going to engage both sides of the brain in the process of reading the sample passage called Dave. Although the entire passage appears below, do not read it yet, but skip down to Instructions for Reading the Sample Practice Reading Comprehension and Memory Passage: "Dave" and let it guide you to read the sample passage in small chunks as directed.

Sample Practice Reading Comprehension and Memory Passage: "Dave"

Dave looked at his watch as he rushed out of his apartment. It was Monday morning and he was late again. As he ran down the steps of his apartment building, heading towards his red sports car, he felt the humid air pressing in on him. It was going to be another hot summer day in June. Dave opened his car door, tossed his brown attaché case onto the passenger seat, and slid into the driver's side. This was the only thing he looked forward to every morning, driving his new car along the freeway to his office. He looked forward to next week when he would begin a two-week vacation.

As he drove towards Interstate 72, his mind raced along thinking about his holiday. Aruba sounds good with its dry air, its seventy-degree weather, and its cool ocean breezes—a change from this stifling humidity, he thought to himself. A short ring from his cell phone startled him out of his daydream.

Instructions for Reading the Sample Passage "Dave": Now, we are going to read through this passage together, using your best superlink memory and learning style and brain style to convert this into an experience that you will save in your long-term memory. As we read, visual people will *see* what is happening, auditory people will *hear* what is happening, tactile people will *feel* what is happening, and kinesthetic people will be experiencing ***doing*** the actions of what is happening.

Ready to roll the scene? You can make it a movie, a theater production, or a real-life event happening to you. Ready? Lights, camera, action:

The passage first says: Dave looked at his watch as he rushed out of his apartment. Make an image in your mind of Dave. Think of someone named Dave that you know, either a personal relationship or an actor, athlete, or someone famous, so you can remember his name. Or, you can become Dave for this movie, and look at your watch. Describe your watch in your Superlinks memory and learning style (Visual learners may see its shape and color; auditory learners may hear it ticking; tactile learners will feel the watch against their wrist; and kinesthetic learners may experience themselves doing an exercise along with the moving of the secondhand of the watch). Next, experience yourself rushing out of your apartment. Based on your superlink memory and learning style you will either imagine: What the apartment looks like? Sounds like? Feels like? What action is going on in the apartment?

Read the next phrase: It was Monday morning.... Think, "How will you remember Monday morning? What images come to you when you think of Monday? How would you portray Monday on a movie screen to let the audience know that it is Monday?" Visual learners may see a calendar with Monday marked. Auditory learners may hear the sound of traffic as they return to work on Monday. Tactile learners may feel tired as they resume their back-to-work schedule after a weekend of leisure. Kinesthetic learners may feel their car speed up and slow down in the stop and go traffic as they drive to work during Monday morning rush-hour traffic. The key is to think of an association that will help you remember the word Monday.

Now read the next phrase: ...and he was late again. See, hear, feel, or experience what it is like to be late again. What is going on inside your mind when you are late? Experiencing yourself feeling the tension of being late, seeing that worried look on your face, hearing yourself berate yourself for taking so long in eating breakfast, or your muscles tightening up in preparation for fighting the good fight in rush-hour traffic.

Continue with the next phrase: As he ran down the steps of his apartment building.... Now imagine (see, hear, feel, or experience) yourself running down the steps of an apartment building. What is the apartment building like? If visual, describe it in full details with its shape and size. If auditory, hear the sounds coming from the apartment building. If tactile, what do the walls feel like or what feelings do you get from the building? If kinesthetic, what actions can you do in the apartment building? What is happening on your movie screen, theater production, or real-life experience?

Next, read: ...heading towards his red sports car... Get a red sports car imaged in your mind.

Think, "What does it look like? How does it sound? What does it feel like to own one and how does it feel to be in it? What do your muscles experience as you drive it?"

...he felt the humid air pressing in on him. Think, "What does it look like when it is humid out? What does it sound like to have humid air pressing in on you? What does it feel like? What do your muscles do when you feel humidity?"

It was going to be another hot summer day in June. Think,

213

"How would you portray to an audience a hot summer day in June? Would you show children in bathing suits running through lawn sprinklers to cool down? What comes to your mind when you think of June? Do you think of someone's birthday? Are you at a June wedding?" Whatever meaningful association you have for June use it. Remember, you want to hook this month into your prior knowledge, or whatever else is already in your head related to June. But don't use my examples—you must make up your own or it will not mean anything to you!

Dave opened his car door... Do you have this image of yourself opening a car door? You will be either seeing it, hearing it, feeling it, or doing it.

…tossed his brown attaché case onto the passenger seat... Image in your mind a brown attaché case either that you own, or one that you saw. Note that you are tossing it onto the passenger seat. Image the passenger seat in your own car or someone's car you know.

...and slid into the driver's side. Do this now.

Slide into the driver's seat of your car. See this, hear this, feel it, or do it.

This was the only thing he looked forward to every morning, driving his new car along the freeway to his office. What would someone look like with this attitude? Do you see him smiling as he gets in? Do you hear him say, "Wow, I can't wait to drive my car along the freeway"? Do you feel the thrill he has driving his new car along the freeway? Do you experience racing that car along the highway?

He looked forward to next week when he would begin a two-week vacation. Visualize yourself getting a vacation in one more week. How does that look, sound, or feel to you? Are you packing your suitcases?

Now, focus on remembering the number two — what images come to your mind for two? Do you *feel* your *two* feet relaxing on a chaise lounge on your holiday? Do you *see two* coconuts fall off a palm tree?

Do you *hear* the sound of *two* hands clapping for joy as you leave on your holiday? Can you feel yourself *jump* off a diving board with your *two* feet? Find an association for the number two that is meaningful to you and experience it in your learning style.

As he drove towards Interstate 72... Another number—72. First experience yourself driving towards the interstate. Experience an interstate you know in your own state. Now, work on the number 72. You can make any number of associations—what happened to you or what happened in the world in 1972? Or take it as 7 and 2. What can you associate with 7 and what do you think of for number 2? Is there something that costs 72 dollars, someone who is 72 years old, some football player who wears number 72? Make the association happen on the interstate so you can connect these two together.

...his mind raced along thinking about his holiday. Imagine yourself thinking about your own holiday as you drive along. Personalize it so you will remember it.

Aruba sounds good with its dry air... Now work on the name, Aruba. What images come to mind for you? Do you see or hear an ad for Aruba on television?

Feel what it would be like to go to Aruba. What would do in Aruba? If you have no images, then take the word itself and think of something you already know that sounds like it or take the word apart and find smaller words that sound like those parts. For example, a-rub-a can be like a ruby—see a red ruby.

Or take the spelling instead of the sound—rub—a rub down on your back as you lay out on the beach. Or connect arid or dry to Aruba and say arid Aruba and experience arid, dry air. What does it look, sound, or feel like, and what do you experience yourself doing in the arid, dry air?

...its seventy-degree weather... Another number—70 degrees. You can connect it with your interstate 72 image and subtract 2 to get 70, or you can think of its own association. Some examples that others have used are: some address with 70, someone who is 70, something that happened in 1970, etc. Experience that 70-degree weather.

...and its cool ocean breezes—a change from this stifling humidity, 'he thought to himself. Now see, hear, feel, or do something in cool ocean breezes. Are you surfing, swimming, sun bathing? Experience the stifling humidity. Do you hear yourself complaining about the humidity? Do you feel sticky? Do you experience yourself jumping in a cold shower to wash off that humidity? Image yourself thinking these thoughts to yourself.

A short ring from his cell phone startled him out of his daydream. Be in your car, and see yourself picking up the cell phone, hear the phone and yourself answering it, feel yourself touching the phone, or experiencing yourself grabbing it and putting it up to your ear. Experience yourself snap back to reality from your daydream.

Now, let us do a practice reading comprehension and memory test to see how much you remember of the story having made it in an experience that happened to you in your mind. Answer the following questions, *without* looking back at the story. The answers are at the end of this section of this chapter, but no peeking or the point of this practice reading comprehension and memory exercise will be lost!

1. Name who this story is about.
2. In what kind of place does he live?
3. What time of day does the story begin?
4. What is the weather like outdoors?
5. What month of the year is it?
6. Where is he going that morning?
7. Is he on time?
8. What kind of car does he own and what color?
9. What route will he take?
10. What is his favorite activity each morning?
11. Where is he thinking about going on vacation?
12. When is he going on his vacation?
13. What is the weather like in the place he is going for his vacation?
14. What is the temperature like in the place he is going for his vacation?
15. What happens to him as he drives to work?

If you imaged the story in your best superlink memory and learning style and brain style as I guided you through the reading, you should have found, as does everyone else who has successfully used this technique, that you were able to answer every question for which you made a strong image in your mind. If you missed any questions, analyze why. Most likely you missed a question because you did not make a strong enough image in your mind or you skipped it without imagining it. It is always fascinating to see that the movie scenes that people do not make are gone from their memory when they try to answer the questions, while the movie scenes they did make pop out as if they really experienced the event for themselves!

If you convert each detail of what you read and hear into this experiential event or movie in your mind, you will be able to put into long-term memory everything you wish. You can do this kind of reading with everything you read, fiction or nonfiction. You can do this with the physical or digital texts, such as the daily newspaper, magazine articles, trade journals, memos, bulletins, interoffice communications, blogs, e-mail, faxes, website, or social media sites. The same technique can work with a novel as well as with science material, technical reading, history, social sciences, health, textbooks in any content area subjects, medical books, training manuals for any field, and anything else you can think of.

The next question you may ask is, "Doesn't it take a long time to read this way?" The reply is, no, it is actually quicker. It only seemed longer because you are just learning the technique and I had to talk you though this initial practice reading comprehension and memory exercise to train you to read or listen in this way. I was guiding you with a series of questions advising you on what to think about as you read, but you will take over from here and begin to ask yourself the questions as you read: What am I seeing (hearing, feeling, or doing) now in my experience or movie? When you think this, it takes only a few seconds. As you practice this technique for several weeks, you will not need to ask the question anymore—you will automatically begin to see, hear, feel, or experience the action as you read. After a few weeks or months, you will find that the moment you read the words, the image appears. Soon, reading will be like a continual movie playing in your head in which you are not even conscious of the words at all. You will actually read faster because you will be immediately experiencing the images and you will move along continually without stopping at phrases anymore. Best of all, you will have increased and improved your memory to read and recall everything you choose!

Memory Improvement Exercise 2: Find something to read on the subject you have chosen to learn. Take two or three paragraphs and practice reading them as shown in the example readings in this chapter. After each phrase, ask yourself what are you seeing (if you are a visual learner), hearing (if you are an auditory learner), feeling, touching, or doing with your hands (if you are a tactile learner), or doing with your large motor muscles or experiencing (if you are a kinesthetic learner). Read the entire passage in that way. Then put the book down and see how many details you can recall, focusing on names, dates, places, and small facts. Practice reading this way with all reading material from now on until you find you can make the movie images automatically, the moment you scan the words.

Answers to questions on the Sample Practice Reading Comprehension and Memory Passage: "Dave":

1) Dave;
2) an apartment or apartment building;
3) morning;
4) humid, or hot and humid;
5) June;
6) to work;
7) no, he is late;
8) red sports car;
9) Interstate 72 or the freeway;

10) driving his car on the freeway (or to work);

11) Aruba;

12) next week;

13) dry air, cool ocean breezes, or seventy-degree weather;

14) seventy degrees;

15) a phone call.

Step 4) Keeping that Memory Active by Retrieving It and Using It

The next step is to make sure the information you read stays in your mind, as an active file, readily accessible at your fingertips, by deciding how often you need to use the information you learned and for what purposes. Think of it as having material immediately accessible on your computer's hard disk as opposed to putting it on flash sticks or thumb drives and filing them somewhere deep in your closet.

There may be certain types of information that are only needed for a one-time purpose. You may need to pass a test or exam and never need that information again. Suppose you took an art history course that was required for your fine arts degree. You do not want to go into art history, but you do want to be an artist. You need the information to pass the test for your degree, but you do not want to load your mind with dates of famous paintings. Thus, you consciously decide to retain that data only so long as you need it to pass the examination and then let it go. You no longer want to work at keeping that memory active. Thus, you do not devote any more attention on it, and you do not use it or retrieve it anymore. Therefore, it is buried by newer, more relevant data that you need to learn.

Step four in training your memory involves making a conscious choice about which long-term memories you wish to keep in an active file and which ones you will allow to be buried in an inactive state. To keep a file active, we need to use it and retrieve it periodically. You may not use the dates of the paintings ever again in your life so you let them go, but if you worked as a tour guide in an art museum, you would use that information again and again. It would become a part of you, and you could instantly bring it from memory, whenever you needed it. If we took a computer course and needed to use what we learned on our jobs every day, we would not want to forget the information after the final examination. By using the information daily, we strengthen the neural network or the interconnections that enable us to perform those functions. Retrieval becomes quicker and more automatic, for when we repeatedly use the information we made a conscious effort to learn; it becomes part of our long-term memory.

Step four requires you to: decide how long you want to keep what you learned as an active long-term memory and when and how often you will need to use what you learned and to make a plan for retrieving and using it regularly. If you decide you need to use it for the one-year in which you will be working at a particular job, then you need to spend time practicing using it, doing something with it, or retrieving it daily, weekly, or several times a week so it is fresh in your mind. Put it on your to-do list. If you are visual, scan the material or some notes you have. If you are auditory, talk about it to others or yourself. If you are tactile, write it or make something with your hands related to the material. If you are kinesthetic, do something with it. This will keep the memory active. The more you use it, the more automatic retrieving this memory will become.

Exercise: Using the subject you are learning as an example to practice the techniques in this book, decide how long you want to retain the information as an active long-term memory; when and how often you will need to use what you learned; and your personal plan for retrieving and using the material regularly.

What about Memorization?

Another kind of memory task is pure memorization, which involves recalling lists of facts and data. If you find you have to memorize information just to pass a test or exam, then you can also use your superlink memory and learning style and brain style to accomplish this task quickly.

I have developed eight different memorization techniques, one for each of the eight superlinks memory and learning styles and brain styles. Try it with a list of data you need to remember. Practice the technique until it becomes automatic.

Take the data you are trying to learn and make associations with something you already know. It can be a word that sounds like or is spelled like the word you need to remember. It may be a person or thing that comes to your mind when you think of that word. You need to make up a movie or story in your mind connecting the new word on the list with the old word. The story should be vivid, humorous, imaginative, or far- out—something that will catch your attention and stay in your mind. People having each of the various superlinks memory and learning styles and brain styles will need to enact their associations into a story in a different way based on their superlink memory style.

The main difference between the left-brain and right-brain memory techniques is that left-brain people will need to remember the list in order. The right-brain people can make the associations without going in order unless this is required for a test or task; then the right- brain people can use the left-brain technique combined with their memory style.

Memorizing Data: Suppose you need to recall the following list of words: cat, house, moon, apple, football. Here is how people with each of the different preferred superlinks memory and learning and brain styles can do it:

Right Brain: Remember the associations without putting them in order.

Left Brain: Remember them in linear order. Here is one way to do it: Take your hands and lay them palms down in front of you. Using your left hand first, count on your fingers, beginning with the pinkie, as follows: pinkie finger is one, ring finger is two, middle finger is three, pointer or index finger is four, and thumb is five. Now you will imagine that you are attaching each of the five words to each of your five fingers, in order, beginning with the word *cat*. You will do it according to one of the following superlinks learning style techniques below:

Visual Technique: You will need to *see* the images and their associations. Here are examples to get you started, but you should make up your own (you will remember the ones you create yourself much better than those given to you by someone else):

1. Connect the cat to your pinkie finger. Make up a story that you can see. Can you see a brown cat licking your pinkie finger? What does the cat look like?
2. Connect the house to your ring finger. Are you getting married and standing in front of the doorway of your house, having your spouse put the ring on your ring finger? See that as vividly as you can.
3. Connect the moon to your middle finger. Can you see yourself balancing the moon on your middle finger, holding it up high?
4. Now link the pointer, or index finger, to the apple. Can you see yourself drawing an apple with a crayon on the tip of your index finger? See the color and shape vividly.
5. Now, link the football to your thumb. See the football hitting your thumb as you try to catch it. Can you see the football bouncing off your thumb and going over the goal post? See the events happening vividly. Now, when you look back at your five fingers, what do you see? Do you remember all the words?

Auditory Technique: You need to hear associations by talking about them, or making up a story that involves the sounds of the words. Here are some examples, but you should create your own that are meaningful to you:

1. Hear the cat meowing as it licks your pinkie finger.
2. You are listening to music in your house as you take off the ring from your ring finger, toss it on the ground, and hear the jangle of the gold on the floor.

3. You are an astronaut in a space ship and you use your middle finger to push a button to aim your ship for the moon, saying, Mission control, we are heading to the moon. Hear the ship's engines boom as you take off.
4. You use your index finger to aim an arrow at an apple, and as you pull back the arrow and let it go, you hear the whiz of it cutting through the air.
5. You hear the shouts from the people in the stadium as you grab that football with your thumb, throw it, and hear it whip through the air to the goalpost.

Another auditory method is to work with the sound of the words as follows:

1. Name the cat on your pinkie finger Pinkie.
2. Ring the bell of your house with your ring finger.
3. Middle finger starts with *m*, and *moon* starts with *m*.
4. Apple and pointer finger both have *p* in them.
5. A baby says fumb, instead of thumb, which reminds you of fumbling the football. Now, when you name each of your five fingers what do you hear?

Do you remember all the words?

Tactile Technique: You are going to feel the sensation and emotions of the associations between the new words and the fingers of your hand.

1. Remember a cat you liked (or did not like). Bring it to your memory. Recall your feelings about that cat. Feel the cat licking your pinkie finger. Stroke the cat's soft fur with your pinkie finger. How does it feel?

2. Recall your favorite house. Now imagine yourself putting a ring on the ring finger of someone you love while in your favorite house. How do you feel?

3. Feel yourself pushing a moon rock with your middle finger. How does the rock feel to you? What is its texture? Is it hard or soft? How does it feel?

4. Remember a favorite type of apple you like to eat. You are mixing applesauce with your pointer finger. How does it feel? Take some with your pointer finger and lick it. How does the texture feel on your tongue? Do you like it?

5. You are gripping the football with your thumb as you play. Feel the ground below your feet as your run towards the goal. Feel the texture of the football. Do you enjoy playing? Now, when you touch each of your five fingers what do you feel? Do you remember all the words?

Kinesthetic Technique: You will need to act out the words:

1. You are a cat and are crawling around on the floor. Take hold of your owner's pinkie finger and pull him or her playfully to romp on the floor with you.

2. You are building a house and in your exercise room you hang ropes with large rings from which to swing. Experience yourself swinging from the rings that are shaped like the ring on your ring finger.

3. You are doing a handstand on the moon, balancing on your middle finger.

4. You are twirling an apple on your pointer finger and tossing it up and down in the air.

5. You catch a football with your thumb and then run to the goal line to make a touchdown. Now, when you flick each of your five fingers what else are you doing? Do you remember all the words?

Mnemonics as a Memory Device for Each Superlink Memory and Learning Style and Brain Style

You can try another memory improvement technique, mnemonics, by using the first letter of each word to make either a new word or a sentence using words that begin with the same first letters as the words in the list. The left-brain people will put the letters in order, while the right-brain people can mix up the order to create other sentences or words.

The **visual people** will *see* the words on paper or a chart or visualize the words in their minds.

The **auditory people** will *hear* and *say* the words or experience themselves saying the words in their minds.

The **tactile people** will *write* the words or imagine themselves feeling the sensation of what the words describe.

The **kinesthetic people** will *stand up and write* the words in large print at a chalk board or white board, or will use big blocks or cut out shapes with the letters on them and move them around. Or they will experience themselves doing an action with the words in their minds.

For example, to remember the five words: *cat, house, moon, apple,* and *football,* here are a left-brain and a right-brain memory improvement technique:

Left-brain people can put the words in order to make the nonsense word: *chmaf*: *c* for *cat*; *h* for *house*; *m* for *moon*; *a* for *apple*; and *f* for *football*. Or they can make a sentence from the first letter of each word: Can *he* *m*ake *a* fire? Added to that can be the actual words as part of the story. Can he make a fire? Have the moon shining over the house, as the cat sitting, on a football, chews an apple by the fire.

Right-brain people can mix-up the order in any way. Since the right side sees all the letters of a word simultaneously and does not put things in sequential order, it can remember them as effectively in any order it likes. For example: cham(p). Replace *f* with *p* and associate the *f* with the word *football*: He was the champ in football.

Another technique is to make a sentence with the first letters of each word arranged in any order: *My friend has a cat*. You can then add the relevant words to this sentence to make a story: While you were sitting in your house, under a full moon, your friend came over with the cat, which was playing with a football and an apple.

The key to improve and increase your memory is to make associations that are meaningful to you, that are out of the ordinary, and that tie the new words to the old words in some way.

Another technique is to connect all the words to make a unified story in which you play an active part. You will do one or a combination of the following based on your superlink learning style and brain style: see the story, hear the story, feel the story, or act out the story in your mind. The following is an example: You and your cat were taken from the house and sent up to the moon. You had apples to eat on the way. When you got to the moon you played football together and it was fun because you could bounce really high.

Improve Memory of Vocabulary Words in English or Other Languages:

Learning any field often requires understanding and recalling new terminology and vocabulary, so this section will be useful to improve memory in many situations. You can use this technique to learn and improve your memory of the meaning of new words, either English or other languages. Remember, the visual learners will make a visual image; the auditory learners will hear and say the words of the association; the tactile learners will feel it; and the kinesthetic learners will do some action with the words.

English Vocabulary Words:
abase: to lower, humiliate
abashed: embarrassed, ashamed

Step 1: Take the word and find another word that looks or sounds like it and is already in your memory bank: Example: abase: sounds like *base*, something that is on the ground.

Step 2: Make up a story connecting the word you already know with the meaning of the new word: for example, I was so humiliated I wanted to sink into the *base* or the ground.

Step 3: Connect the story with your superlink memory and learning style and brain style. Visual learners will see themselves with humiliated looks on their faces, sinking down to the base, or floor. Auditory learners will hear themselves saying they are humiliated and hear the crash as they fall to the base, or floor.

Tactile learners will feel themselves being humiliated and feel themselves touch the base, or floor. Kinesthetic learners will be playing a basketball game and when they lose, they are humiliated and will fall down on the base, or floor.

When you see or hear the word *abase* in the story you created, the word will replay like a movie in your head and the concept of humiliation and lowering will come up as a movie scene, giving you its meaning.

Let's try the next word: abashed: ashamed. The word *abashed* sounds and looks like *bashed*. When you bashed into the wall because you weren't looking, you were ashamed. See it, hear it, feel it, or do it based on your superlink memory and learning style and brain style, and the word is yours.

Words in other languages: The same principle can be used for learning how to learn and improve your memory and vocabulary for words in different languages. For example: Here are steps if you want to remember the French word *maison,* which means house.

Step 1: Think of a word that sounds like, looks like, or is similar to *maison*, or the parts of the word: May's son; my son; maize or corn; May sun.

Step 2: Make up a story connecting the association with the meaning of the word. Let's take May sun. Link the hot May sun in the sky and your house. You might come up with a sentence such as, The May sunshine was beating down on my house.

Step 3: Connect the story with your superlink memory and learning style. Visual learners will see it, auditory learners will hear it, tactile learners will feel it, and kinesthetic learners will act it out.

Let us try an example with a Spanish word *blanco*, which means white. Connect *blanco* to a blank sheet of paper that is white. Now you have *blanco* as white.

A Trained Memory Accelerates Learning

By improving your memory, you can learn something correctly the first time and cut down the wasted study time rereading and restudying the same material. You can accelerate your learning by training your memory using your superlink memory and learning style and brain style.

CHAPTER 22:
APPLYING WHAT YOU HAVE LEARNED ABOUT IMPROVING MEMORY TO ACHIEVE YOUR GOALS

With continual new discoveries about our brain, our concepts of education, memory, and learning are rapidly changing. With the information explosion, we have access to every bit of information that exists in the world today. As our education system catches up to current technology, we will find that learning is not only memorization of textbooks in order to pass tests. We will discover that learning is also a process of fulfilling our goals and dreams and contributing to making the world a more humane, more peaceful, and more satisfying place to live. Learning can become a tool for the attainment of our individual and collective destinies.

As we realize that we have only a given number of years to live and enough information in the world to occupy us for many lifetimes we will need to make choices as to what we want to remember and for what purpose. No one has the time to recall everything there is to know. We must accept that fact and decide what portion of that vast ocean of knowledge we want to own. It will not be the same for everyone. As we have seen, people have different interests and talents. In this book, we have seen the vast differences that exist between the eight types of learners and the combinations of Superlinks memory and learning styles and brain styles and how our own unique skills contribute to the diversity and talent pool required to make this world function.

Each superlink memory and learning style and brain style plays a part in human interdependence and each memory style is as valuable as the next. We need to honor and respect our differences and use our combined talents to solve mutual problems facing our planet.

We will need to take charge of our own learning, memory techniques, and education. As the job market changes with each new technological discovery, we need to keep pace with it and decide what we need to know, when we need to know it, and for what purpose. We will rely more and more on self-study and self-learning as we strive to compete with this ever-changing panorama of the modern world. We not only need to learn this for ourselves, but we need to teach these tools to children so they can be ready for whatever world faces them when they grow up.

The knowledge you gained in this book can empower you with the skill of knowing how to remember any subject quickly and to master it. To date, this is the current technology available to us. With each passing year, more research findings and newer technologies will provide us with still more ways to improve our memory. Who knows—one day, we may have microchips or a pill with a memory chip implanted in us from which we can access all the world's knowledge! We need to always stay open to new discoveries and new findings and add it to our existing knowledge to move forward. Until those new technologies are accessed, you have the memory tools in this book a tool that can empower you to remember any subject in the shortest possible time. If you did the practice exercises, you would already have used these memory tools to work through one subject that you selected as a practice case.

In the beginning of this book, you selected a subject to remember as you worked through the activities. You also had a goal or purpose for remembering that subject. Think back to what that goal was. If you worked through all these practice activities, you would be well on your way to mastering your subject by using the memory tools provided in the book. You can now apply this to remember other subjects.

Take a moment and list other areas that you would like to remember. Then, go through all the exercise pages in the book to complete your personal plan for remembering each of these subjects.

Many people think of learning as a dead-end road. They learn something and that is the end of it. Few people actually *use* what they learn. Many people take courses and never apply the material or skills they have learned to their lives. Twelve years of schooling, possibly sixteen or more if we go to training schools, colleges, or higher education, have conditioned us into taking courses, passing tests, and forgetting the material the following day. As a society, we have come to equate learning with passing tests and getting grades, diplomas, or certificates. However, the true nature of learning is a transformation into a better self, a higher self, a fully-developed self. As a by-product, we can put what we learned into the service of humanity at large and make the world a better place. Using our memory is a tool to help us achieve our goals and dreams.

The final step in improving memory is to apply what we learned to our everyday lives. That is the best and fastest way to crown our learning, to ensure our mastery of the subject. Having reached the point where we have mastered a subject, we want to gain experience by applying what we remembered to real-life situations. By doing so, we move forward on our life's journey to meet the goals we have set for ourselves.

If we are learning a skill for a current job or hobby, we are most likely going to apply what we learned on a regular basis. If we have learned and remembered material in a new subject unrelated to our current activities, the following are some examples of how we can apply these to everyday life:

Literature: Continue to read on your own; start a discussion group; keep a journal; and do your own writing.

Sports or dance: Find some friends or join a group to practice a sport or dance.

Using the Internet: Spend time daily surfing to locate websites related to your interests.

Carpentry: Start a small project, building something for your home or family or friends

Cooking: Invite friends over for a gourmet meal.

Marketing: Take a product your business produces and improve on marketing it.

Health: Set some personal health goals in the areas of diet, nutrition, fitness, or exercise; start a personal program for yourself or join a fitness club.

Quantum Physics: Find a laboratory to visit or work in, either part-time or as a volunteer so you can apply what you learned to research; join a book study group on the subject.

Learning is more than studying for a test. Having passed our examinations or performance assessments and proven our memory of a subject or skill, we do not want to have wasted all that time and let our knowledge fade away with disuse. True, there may be subjects we had to take for which we had no use. Focus instead on those subjects that you chose to study as part of your life's work, goals, interests, hobbies, or talents. The process of memory is complete when we use what we learned right away.

In the past, learners used to do tons of practice activities, yet did not recall the subject when they were assessed months later because they did not apply what they learned. When they used their knowledge and skills in everyday life the material stayed in their long-term memory. The final stage in increasing your memory of a subject is to use what you recalled in your daily life.

Improving Memory Begins Early

Jerome Bruner, the great educationist, taught that anything can be taught to anyone at any age if taught at his or her level. This one statement that I read when I was in college has guided my entire teaching career, and I have found it to prove true time and time again. By using the technology in this book, you can begin improve the memory of children from birth.

We have a misconception in our society that the very young and very old are living in a state, unaware of what is happening around them. We let children lie in cribs or carriages for hours, unstimulated with no one to talk to them, no one to provide them with challenges, no one to expose them to life. For each hour they lie awake doing nothing, they lose an hour of learning time. It is the same with the elderly who are left to sit with nothing to do.

Learning begins at birth. When we expose children to mental stimuli in infancy and their toddler years, we help them develop talents and abilities early. From infancy, we can develop their whole brain, both left and right sides, and all four memory and learning styles, visual, auditory, tactile, and kinesthetic, by exposing them to a rich environment filled with stimuli in each modality. We need not wait until age five, when they enter kindergarten. As a society, we need to extend education and memory training to infancy, training parents and communities to provide opportunities for early stimulation. Having work with gifted students, I found that a common thread in each of their upbringings was that their parents provided them with early language experiences, early reading experiences, and a wide range of experiences in math, science, music, art, sports, and hobbies as babies and toddlers.

Those children who are identified as gifted and talented or who have high IQs (intelligence quotients) are not necessarily genetically endowed; part of it is due to their upbringing—to what stimulus they were exposed. When I worked with gifted students I used to question their parents as to what they did with their children during their infancy to find out what was the significant difference between them and the children who were not in gifted programs. The one common thread among each of their upbringing was that their parents talked to them from birth, as if adults, and discussed everything with them. In some cases, the parents exposed them to math concepts, books, writing, drawing, science, the arts, music, athletics, crafts, vocational skills, and hundreds of other skills. Whatever the child was exposed to in infancy and their toddler years, they already showed talent and ability even in kindergarten, first, second, and third grades. Also, giftedness spans a wide range of talent—for some it may be scoring high on a test of verbal abilities, for others it may be nonverbal abilities, and for many it could be gifted in art, music, sports, or a hobby. The early exposure to develop the brain networks for a particular talent grows those neuron connections to cause someone to excel in a particular area. It confirmed for me the fact that whatever we expose a child to he or she will learn and remember. I founded National Reading Diagnostics Institute to teach memory techniques to accelerate learning to help learners improve in memory, reading comprehension, listening comprehension, study skills, note taking, and test-taking skills. I have consistently seen children from pre-school, kindergarten, and first grade through twelfth grade, college, and adults accelerate their reading and math abilities by an average of two to five years' growth in as short a time as two to eight months. Anyone *can* learn how to remember anything quickly by using the accelerated plan provided. If we teach young people how to improve their memory, we will see a nation of students who are ready for higher level work at earlier ages, instead of finding upper grade students and adults dropping out of society because no one has taught them *how* to remember and learn.

Maturity Is No Barrier to Improving Memory

Just as young people can be trained in the methods of memory improvement, so can mature citizens. Studies have shown that our brain does not decline after retirement. We have sentenced millions of people in their 70s, 80s, 90s, and 100s or older into believing that their days of learning and remembering are over. You read earlier in the book that increased stimulation from our senses to the brain causes the development of our nerve cells and their interconnections necessary for continued brain growth and development. That development continues all through our life. It is society that promotes the false belief that our development is over when we retire. A study was conducted by the National Institute of Aging on ninety- and hundred-year old nuns in Mankato, Minnesota.

Hundreds of them had donated their brains to research after they died to see whether the stimulation of their mind with mental exercise caused their brain cells to branch out, adding more connections between brain cells. In their later years, the study showed that those nuns had continued to learn and developed their minds and did not seem to suffer from dementia, Alzheimer's, and other debilitating brain diseases as early or as severely as the general population. (from Building a Better Brain, by Daniel Golden, *National Geographic*, June 1994, p. 63-70.)

We do not have to stop using our memory powers when we graduate school, or when we retire. Learning and remembering can be a lifelong pursuit, bringing with it new skills, new interests, new hobbies, new talents, and new contributions to the lives of people around us and the world. We can choose to take continuing education courses from others and can recall them in an accelerated way, or we can plan an accelerated program of self-study using the memory tools in this book. Live each day as if a new life is ahead of us. Age is an illusion. Decide to wake up each day as fresh and vibrant as you did as a child, teen, or young adult, looking forward to your entire life ahead of you. Many talented and gifted writers, scientists, artists, inventors, musicians, and craftspeople began their careers after sixty or seventy! You can, too!

Teaching Others to Improve Memory

One of the best ways to learn a subject is to teach it to others. To teach, you must digest the subject, make it a part of you, and then express it in your own ways to others. By doing so, you become familiar with the subject and, over time, even become an expert in the subject. Take the subject you have studied and try to teach it to someone else. It does not have to be formal instruction. You can share what you learned about memory improvement and the subject you learned with a family member, a friend, a child, or a co-worker who is interested in the same subject. Find out their Superlinks memory and learning style and brain style and teach it to them in their best memory style.

You can even share the knowledge about memory improvement that you gained in this book with someone. People love to hear about themselves. Share the knowledge you gained about Superlinks memory and learning styles and brain styles and improving memory with friends, family, and co-workers as a way to reinforce in your mind what you have learned. This will help make the information a lasting part of yourself as well.

Changing Yourself and the World

You have invested time in reading this book and working through it. Now that you have completed this book and the area of study you used as an example to learn these memory techniques, you have that time freed up so you can put what you learned to use. You can apply these memory techniques to learn any other field you wish to learn. Can you help yourself with that knowledge? Can you help someone else? Can you use it at your job? Can you use it to help your family? Can you use it to solve a problem in your community, nation, or the world? Can you use it to help students improve their memory in schools, colleges, or any educational institution?

Exercise: Think about the subject you chose to remember as you worked through this book. List all the ways that you can apply what you learned and remembered to your daily life, using what you learned for your personal transformation, to help others, or to transform the world:

Take Action for Your Own Personal Transformation, the Attainment of Your Dreams, and Making the World a Better Place

It is time that we move out of the dark ages and into the age of enlightenment of how to improve memory to keep pace with the times. By knowing the tools for how to remember anything quickly, you will be able to apply the skills and knowledge much quicker to achieve your own personal transformation and in transforming the world. Applying what you learned can lead to your achieving your life's goals.

BONUS FOR READERS

How to Find Your Fastest Way to Improve Memory: How to Take the Superlinks Learning Style Inventory Test: Linksman Learning Style Preference Assessment™ and Linksman Brain Hemispheric Preference Assessment™

If you wish to find your best and fastest way of remembering by taking the Superlinks Learning Style and Brain Style Inventory, consisting of the Linksman Learning Style Preference Assessment™ and Linksman Brain Hemispheric Preference Assessments,™ a simple, quick online memory and learning style and brain style assessment inventory that is automatically scored, giving instant results in a personalized report, you can go to any of the following three websites: www.superlinkslearning.com or www.readinginstruction.com, or www.keystoreadingsuccess.com which is the accelerated program of K-12, college and adult reading, memory, note taking, study, and test-taking skills. The superlinks test is the same whether taken through either of these 3 Internet sites. There is an English and Spanish version of the tests, with more languages soon to be available. The assessment on the Keys to Reading Success™ website also contains a pre-K, kindergarten, Grade 1 through Grade 12, college, and adult reading diagnostic test, instantly scored with a prescriptive reading plan to accelerate learning, plus lessons to improve reading comprehension, memory, study skills, phonics, fluency, vocabulary, and test-taking for reading in any content area subject through each of the brain's eight Superlinks memory and learning styles and brain styles or your fastest way of remembering. Lessons have adaptations for all superlinks memory and learning styles and brain hemispheric preference styles. It contains an entire reading comprehension, memory, study, and test-taking skills curriculum for any age, whether for pre-K, kindergarten, Grade 1 through Grade 12, college, or adult, in each of the superlinks learning styles and brain hemispheric preference styles.

Once you take the Superlinks memory and learning style and brain style test, you will get your results and a detailed report on how you learn and remember the best, what materials you need, what is the best learning environment, what is the best memory strategies, and how you best communicate with others and want others to communicate with you.

Find Your Own and Other People's Fastest and Best Way of Improving Memory

You can go to the website to get a license to take the online version of the Superlinks test. **Note:** Use the special discount code provided to the readers of this book, *How to Improve Memory Quickly by Knowing Your Personal Memory Style: Quick, Easy Tips to Improve Memory through the Brain's Fastest Superlinks Memory and Learning Style*. The discount will give you access to the test at a nominal fee from the usual cost for the test. To access a license to take the test, go to: http://www.readinginstruction.com and select from the Explore Learning Store: Superlinks to Accelerated Learning™ Assessment and enter the discount code: HTLAQ or contact info@keyslearning.com Note: At checkout, the discount will be entered and applied to reduce the cost.

If you are a teacher, parent, coach, trainer, sports coach, employer, or someone who wishes to have students, trainees, employees, athletes, or group members take the test to find their best way of remembering, you can get bulk licenses at special rates by contacting info@keyslearning.com.

It will score the results for you instantly and automatically and give you an instant personalized report of your best Superlink memory style. From there, go to the chapter that describes your Superlinks memory and learning style and brain style to begin using the revolutionary brain-based approach for remembering any subject fast.

ABOUT THE AUTHOR:
RICKI LINKSMAN

Ricki Linksman is the author and developer of one of the fastest brain-based memory improvement, accelerated learning, learn to read, improve reading comprehension, and learn anything quickly programs in the world today. She is the author of many books, including *How to Learn Anything Quickly: Quick, Easy Tips to Improve Memory, Reading, Comprehension, Test-Taking, and Learning through the Brain's Fastest Superlinks Learning Style*; *The Fine Line between ADHD and Kinesthetic Learners: 197 Kinesthetic Activities to Quickly Improve Reading, Memory, and Learning in Just 10 Weeks: The Ultimate Parent Handbook for ADHD, ADD, and Kinesthetic Learners*; *How to Improve Memory Quickly by Knowing Your Personal Memory Style: Quick, Easy Tips to Improve Memory through the Brain's Fastest Superlinks Memory and Learning Style*; From ADHD to A's: How to Improve Reading, Memory, and Learning Quickly for Kinesthetic Learners; Kinesthetic Vocabulary Activities; *Your Child Can Be a Great Reader*; and *Solving Your Child's Reading Problems*, featured in *Publisher's Weekly, Women's World, Family Life, Chicago Parent, Chicago Tribune, Los Angeles Parent, San Diego Parent*, the *Naperville Sun*, and the *Lisle Sun*. She has written numerous other books on accelerated learning and reading comprehension. Superlinks has been applied to accelerating and improving learning to golf, in the book, co-written by past president of the LPGA, Kerry Graham, and Ricki Linksman, called *The Power of Mental Golf*.

Ricki Linksman is also the founder-director of National Reading Diagnostics Institute, headquartered in Naperville, Illinois, near Chicago, a training institution to help people of all ages to accelerate learning and improve their memory through Superlinks™, a system she developed using neuroscience and brain research, learning styles, and brain styles. Through Ricki Linksman's methods, people can improve their performance on their job and in their studies. By improving comprehension and memory of what they read, people can excel in any field. She runs a training institution in which trainers, sports and life coaches, instructors, administrators, employers, and teachers in any field can learn how to be more effective in training employees, students, and trainees.

She also directs a parent center in which she offers reading diagnostic testing and learning style and brain style inventory assessments to find one's fastest way of learning and remembering. Through diagnostic testing her methods include developing an individual prescriptive plan followed by coaching, teaching, and tutoring students from pre-K, kindergarten, Grades 1 through Grades 12, college, to adult learners. Students show dramatic improvement whether they are in regular education, special education, Title 1, remedial reading, have ADHD or ADD, are in bilingual or ESOL, ELL, ESL, or dual language programs, or who are gifted. She was the developer of one of the first parent involvement programs in the country, and was featured in Cendant and Davidson's Reading Blaster™ 9-12 popular software program as creating a Parent Tips guidebook, and was chosen as one of the best reading experts in the country to consult in the production of Cendant's *Learn to Read*™ software package.

At National Reading Diagnostics Institute, parents are trained how to accelerate their children's or teens' memory and learning. Her Keys to Reading Success™ program includes parent involvement worksheets to help parents be more effective in providing homework help.

Ricki has been serving students in public and private schools throughout the country and around the world. Whenever she has set up the system of accelerated learning and accelerated reading in schools, those schools have raised test scores and achievement through her memory methods within less than one school year. Test scores raised include CTBS, SAT, ACT, and ISAT (Illinois State Achievement Test). Her memory improvement program has also been used to prepare students for career examinations in diverse fields, such as medicine and law.

Ricki Linksman is also the developer of *Keys to Reading Success*, an Internet-based pre-K, kindergarten, grades 1 through 12, and college reading program to use accelerated learning and memory techniques and learning styles and brain hemispheric preference strategies to teach students to learn to read or improve reading within four to eight months or less. The average success rate is 98-99% of all K-12 students using the program rise 2-5 grade levels in reading in 6-8 months, including students in regular education, special education, ELL, ESL, ESOL, bi-lingual and dual language, Title 1 or Remedial Reading, and gifted programs (and those with ADD or ADHD).

Rusty Acree, a retired veteran and current football referee, of Richmond, Virginia, is one of many parents and grandparents who have seen the effectiveness of the program on his grandson. His grandson, who had been previously labeled with ADHD, had been left back in kindergarten for two years, yet still could neither recognize the letters of the alphabet nor read a word. When he was diagnosed by Ricki as a kinesthetic right- brain learner and was taught how to read through his kinesthetic right-brain Superlinks style he was able to learn the letters of the alphabet and could read his first book ever within 2 days. Rusty Acree who continued to see the phenomenal growth of his grandson over the next year to get to grade level in reading has called Ricki Linksman, The Michael Jordan of Reading.

Ricki developed the *Superlinks to Accelerated Learning* program with its *Linksman Learning Style Preference Assessment and Brain Hemispheric Preference Assessment*, 'used to discover a person's best memory Superlink (learning style and brain style) to accelerate learning.

Her programs Keys to Reading Success™ and Superlinks to Accelerated Learning™ were selected by a foundation, the Cotchery Foundation, started by New York Jets football running back, Jericho Cotchery and his wife Mercedes Cotchery, to assist an elementary school in North Carolina raise its reading scores and is featured on the Cotchery Foundation website.

Her award-winning phonics program has been selected for use as the phonics curriculum used by Huntington™ Learning Centers throughout the country. Other companies that have used her Superlinks to Accelerated Learning™ programs include Kaplan On-line University; MFS Investment Management, Boston, a large Massachusetts financial institution who used Ricki Linksman's accelerated learning techniques to help trainers teach clients about mutual funds sales; and by one of the largest technology company in the world.

Recently, Ricki Linksman created a phonics program called Off the Wall Phonics™ specially designed for kinesthetic and tactile learners, but can be used with visual and auditory learners also, including those with a right-brain or left- brain preference. It allows students to learn to master and remember every phonics patterns in the English language to move someone from beginning reading to college-level word reading ability within 10 game levels, of 10 games each. If followed, any student can raise their word-reading level, which can help their reading comprehension, by playing one game level per week for ten weeks, and studies have proven the average raise in word-reading level to be two to five grade levels in reading in that time.

A university football team used Keys to Reading Success™ and Superlinks to Accelerated Learning™ to improve football performance through learning and memory styles and brain styles, helping them to their first winning season. It dramatically changed the way football coaches taught football playbooks to the athletes.

She has worked as a consultant to golf instructors to improve teaching of golf through Superlinks to Accelerated Learning™ learning styles. She was a consultant to a former White Sox baseball player on product development of a pitching aid to improve pitching skills using Superlinks to Accelerated Learning™. As a trainer of trainers, she has improved the effectiveness of trainers to help them reach participants of different learning styles.

Four schools and educational institutions in South Africa from elementary school to a college, (including Reading Identity, Learning Identity, Clifton Preparatory School, Oasis Preparatory School, Durban, Cowan House, and Hilton

College), have adopted Keys to Reading Success and Superlinks to Accelerated Learning to improve memory and reading.

Ricki works as a consultant to businesses, companies, and educational institutions to help people accelerate and improve memory and learning in any field. She has done trainings for college professors and instructors at colleges and universities. She has also done volunteer work training tutors for Literacy Volunteers for America. She trained facilitators for youth outreach programs sponsored by a local police station and worked with students from DCFS (Department of Children and Family Services). She has also served as a reading expert for a pro-bono court case for a major Chicago law firm. Public schools call on Ricki Linksman's expertise on case study teams for students.

She has run Administrator Academies in Illinois on District Reading Improvement, training superintendents and principals in steps to improve their district reading programs and scores. She has been one of the trainers for Illinois's ISAT (Illinois State Achievement Test) reading and writing tests and has trained teachers in how to raise test scores on this state test. She was one of Illinois's state validators for the Right to Reading Initiative. She has presented memory and learning strategies to many Regional Offices of Education to train teachers and administrators from many school districts in these methods.

She gives seminars and workshops, appears at book-signings, and speaks at conferences. She has presented her memory improvement and reading programs to tens of thousands of teachers across the country. She works as a consultant and trainer for public school districts and schools in accelerated learning techniques, raising district reading scores, and improving student achievement. She received a certificate of merit from the IASCD (Illinois Association for Supervision and Curriculum) 1999 Winn Research Award for Maximizing School Reading Scores.

She receives thousands of letters and emails from teachers, administrators, parents, college professors, consultants, and students from all over the world who have read her books and write to her for advice on improving memory, reading, and learning performance. Her works are cited on numerous Internet sites listing excellent resources for parents and teachers, including *Conde Nast.*

She has taught graduate education courses in reading, and another on inclusion: differentiated learning to teach to all learners through learning styles. Specializing in accelerated learning and memory improvement with application to reading, she has taught these techniques to students of all ages and to adults.

For parents and teachers, she has numerous books, EBooks, courses, online e-courses, podcasts, webinars, teleseminars, coaching, and consulting to accelerate learning for all types of learners, including kinesthetic, tactile, auditory, visual, with either a right-brain or left-brain preference. These materials have helped children and teens from pre-K, kindergarten, grade 1-12, and college, whether in regular education, special education, gifted, ESOL, ELL, ESL, bilingual or dual language, or Title 1 or Reading Remedial programs, or those who have ADHD or ADD.

CONTACT INFORMATION

Ricki Linksman can be contacted at:
National Reading Diagnostics Institute and Keys Learning,
Naperville, Illinois;

Email: info@keyslearning.com

Web sites:
http://www.readinginstruction.com
http://www.keyslearning.com
http://www.keystoreadingsuccess.com
http://www.superlinkslearning.com
http://www.nationalreadingdiagnosticsinstitute.com
http://www.offthewallphonics.com

A SPECIAL GIFT FOR READERS

The author has a special gift for readers of this book, *How to Improve Memory Quickly by Knowing Your Personal Memory Style: Quick, Easy Tips to Improve Memory through the Brain's Fastest Superlinks Memory and Learning Style.* If you would like to find your Superlinks memory and learning style and brain hemispheric preference style, or that of your family, friends, and others, as a special reader of *How to Improve Memory Quickly by Knowing Your Personal Memory Style: Quick, Easy Tips to Improve Memory through the Brain's Fastest Superlinks Memory and Learning Style*, here is your special discount code to access the test at a significant discount. Go to: http://www.readinginstructiom.com and from the Explore Learning Store, select Superlinks to Accelerated Learning™ Assessment and enter the discount code: HTLAQ

Note: When you get to the check-out page, scroll down to enter your discount code and the discounted price will appear at check-out. After taking the test, it will instantly be scored and give you a personalized report on your best memory Superlink learning style and brain style with tips on how to improve memory quickly. You can return to the matching chapter in this book to read about how you can improve memory quickly through your Superlinks memory and learning style and brain style and improve your own or others' memory.

Enjoy the rewards of personal transformation!

www.ingramcontent.com/pod-product-compliance
Lightning Source LLC
Chambersburg PA
CBHW060007100426
42740CB00010B/1421